EARLY MARRIAGES FROM NEWSPAPERS PUBLISHED IN CENTRAL NEW YORK

By William M. Beauchamp
Selected and Arranged by Grace Beauchamp Lodder
of the Syracuse Public Library

with an appendix:

MANLIUS, NEW YORK OBITUARIES AND MARRIAGES IN THE EARLY 1800s

Supplied by
H.C. Durston, Village Historian, Manlius, New York

Edited by
MARY KEYSOR MEYER

HERITAGE BOOKS
2007

HERITAGE BOOKS
AN IMPRINT OF HERITAGE BOOKS, INC.

Books, CDs, and more—Worldwide

For our listing of thousands of titles see our website
at
www.HeritageBooks.com

Published 2007 by
HERITAGE BOOKS, INC.
Publishing Division
65 East Main Street
Westminster, Maryland 21157-5026

Copyright © 1992 Mary Keysor Meyer

All rights reserved. No part of this book may be reproduced or transmitted in any form or by any means, electronic or mechanical, including photocopying, recording or by any information storage and retrieval system without written permission from the author, except for the inclusion of brief quotations in a review.

International Standard Book Number: 978-1-58549-832-7

TABLE OF CONTENTS

Introduction v

Sources quoted vii

Map of New York State ix

Map of Central New York State x

Geographical Locator Guide xi

Marriage Records of Central New York 1

Manlius, NY Obituaries and Marriages in Early 1800's 71

Index 87

INTRODUCTION

Dr. William Martin Beauchamp, a native of Orange County, NY, born in 1830, moved with his parents to Skaneateles, New York, at the age of one year. His interest in early newspapers of the area was undoubtedly sparked by the fact that his father, William Millet Beauchamp, commenced publication of *The Skaneateles Democrat* in 1840. Beauchamp entered the ministry and became Rector of Grace Episcopal Church in Baldwinsville, NY, a position he held until his retirement in 1900.

Dr. Beauchamp had a life long interest in local history and genealogy and in 1889 became a Director of the Onondaga Historical Association, a position he held until his death in 1925. In addition to his interest in local history and genealogy, his consuming interest seemed to lie in the field of archaeology and he was for some years New York State Archaeologist with a particular interest in the Indians of the State.

Dr. Beauchamp's daughter, Grace Beauchamp Lodder absorbed some of her father's many interests and for a number of years headed the Local History and Genealogy Department of the Syracuse, NY Public Library. It is to her we owe our gratitude for having transcribed the records which follow, thereby preserving them for future generations.

This work was originally published without an introduction and without an explanation as to just how it came into being, or just exactly what it was. The title of the work gives us some hint as to what it was and how it originated. As we worked with the various entries we came to have some understanding of what we saw.

We believe Dr. Beauchamp copied these records over a long period of time as his method varied considerably. In copying from one newspaper, he consistently noted the issue date of the newspaper, whereas he neglected to do so with the others. We believe the dates appearing in parenthesis are very likely the date the marriage occurred, as deduced by counting backward from the day of issue of the newspaper to the day of the week the marriage took place.

We do not believe he abstracted all pertinent information from the marriage notices. In the majority of instances, the name of the officiating clergyman does not appear. Our experience with early newspaper notices of marriage, leads us to believe that although the names of those ministers were undoubtedly given in most instances, Dr. Beauchamp failed to copy them: items that could lead the reader to another most important source of information - the church record/religious denomination.

The editor suggests that the reader attempt to locate a copy of the actual newspaper (most are available on inter-library loan through the New York State Library in Albany, NY) and look at the original entry.

It is apparent that these abstracts were made in cursive writing, and that Mrs. Lodder could not always decipher his handwriting. Sometimes she would place a question mark to indicate her confusion and at other times she completely misunderstood it.

Despite these shortcomings, the researcher of Central New York families will find this work of great value due to the fact that the State of New York did not require marriage licenses at that time. Marriage records for these early years exist only in newspapers of the time, church records, and family Bibles. The area covered in this work, Onondaga, Madison, Cortland, Cayuga, and Oswego counties for the most part, as well some scattered records state-wide, contribute to its usefulness. Names of principal parties are in alphabetical order; secondary names are indexed.

In addition to Dr. Beauchamp's work, we have included a short compilation of marriage and death notices taken from some early Manlius, NY newspapers. Manlius, a small village east of Syracuse, is within the bounds of Onondaga county and it seemed appropriate to include them.

These records, according to the legend on the front page of the original copy, were transcribed by the N.Y.A. and "furnished" by H. C. Durston, the Manlius Village Historian. Harry C. Durston was appointed historian of Manlius village in November 1937 and continued in that office at least until 1 July 1940 when he was appointed Onondaga County Historian. He held the latter position until his death around 1950. We might therefore set the date of transcription between those dates. However, it is also possible the transcription was made some years earlier and that he found them at the time he assumed the position of Manlius Town Historian.

Whatever the case may be, they are a valuable addition to this book of Central New York records.

                                      Mary Keysor Meyer, F.N.G.S.
                                                            Editor

SOURCES OF INFORMATION

The following newspapers were used by Dr. Beauchamp as a source for the marriage notices included in this work. The initials preceding each entry are the codes used to identify each newspaper.

AFP - *Auburn Free Press* was published in Cayuga county from 1824 to 1833 when it was united with the *Cayuga Republican*.

CP - *The Cayuga Patriot* was started at Auburn in 1814 and continued until 1847 under that name.

OD - *Onondaga Democrat* was started in 1846. After one year it was sold and the name was changed.

OG - *The Onondaga Gazette* was established at Onondaga Hill in 1818 and continued until 1821 when the name was changed to the *Onondaga Journal*. Two years later, another newspaper called the *Onondaga Gazette* commenced publication in Syracuse. In about a year, the name was changed to the *Syracuse Gazette and General Advertiser*.

OR - *Onondaga Register* was established at Onondaga Hollow in 1814 and continued until 1829 when it was moved to Syracuse where it joined the *Onondaga Gazette* and continued publication as the *Onondaga Register and Syracuse Gazette*.

SA - *Syracuse Advertiser* commenced publication in 1825 and continued until 1829 when it was united with the *Onondaga Journal* and the name changed to the *Onondaga Standard*.

SC - *Skaneateles Columbian* was first published in 1831 and continued until 1853.

SD - *Skaneateles Democrat* was commenced in 1840 by William M. Beauchamp, and continued until after 1860.

SFP - *Skaneateles Free Press* - no record but find *The Citizen's Press* published in Onondaga Hollow a short time in 1832.

SG - *Syracuse Gazette* - founded in 1825 and continued until 1829.

SG&GA - *Syracuse Gazette and General Advertiser* commenced about 1824 and continued until 1829.

ST - *Skaneateles Telegraph* was started in 1829 but only a few years.

SW - *Syracuse Whig* published in Syracuse under this name from 1835 to 1837.

ADDITIONAL SOURCES

STJ - The only non-newspaper source used by Dr. Beauchamp in his work was the records of the St. James Protestant Episcopal Church in Skaneateles, NY.

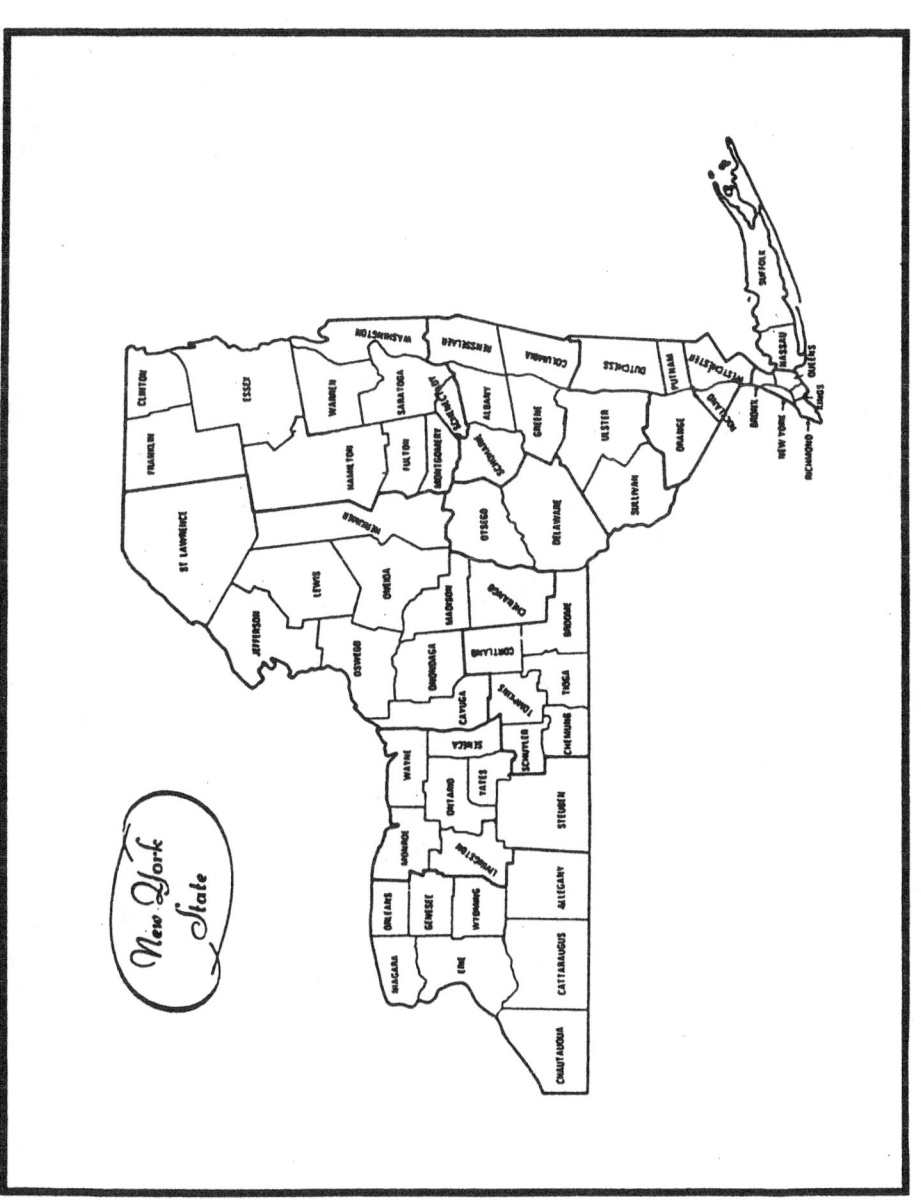

Central New York State

GEOGRAPHICAL LOCATOR GUIDE

Inasmuch as many readers will not be familiar with all the placenames appearing in this work nor will they have immediate access to necessary finding aids, the following locator guide has been developed for their convenience.

We must assume the majority of names of villages, towns, etc. used in this work are located in Onondaga County or the adjacent counties of Madison, Cayuga, Oswego, or Cortland unless otherwise stated.

The following authorities were consulted for names of geographical locations included herein: *J. H. French, Gazetteer of the State of New York...* (Syracuse, NY, 1860); *Bishop Davenport, A New Gazetteer or Geographical Dictionary of North American and the West Indies* (Baltimore, MD, 1835); and *Lippincott's Pronouncing Gazetteer of the World* (Philadelphia, 1895). These early gazetteers were used as many of the villages named no longer appear on a map or have a post office.

As a matter of convenience, the following abbreviations are used:

h.	- hamlet
c.	- city
ca	- circa
ck.	- creek
co.	- county
s.	- island
l.	- locality
mi.	- miles
p.o.	- post office
v.	- village
s.	- settlement
t.	- town/township
v.	- village

The reader should bear in mind that in New York State, the word "town" denotes a township.

PLACES NAMED

Amboy - v. in t. of Camillus, Onondaga Co., NY
Amber - v. in t. of Otisco, Onondaga Co., NY
Albany - c. and co. in NY; capital of NY state
Antwerp - t. and v. in Jefferson Co., NY
Arcadia - t. and v. in Wayne Co., NY
Auburn - c. and county seat, Cayuga Co., NY
Aurora - v. in t. of Ledyard, Cayuga Co., NY
Aurelius - t. and v. in Cayuga Co., NY
Baldwinsville - v. in t. Van Buren Onondaga Co. NY
Ballston - t. and v. in Saratoga Co., NY
Batavia - c. in Genesee Co., NY
Bath - t. and v. in Steuben Co., NY
Belle Isle - v. in t. of Camillus, Onondaga Co. NY
Benton - t. and v. in Yates Co., NY
Beuna Vista - Mexico
Borodino - v. in t. of Spafford, Onondaga Co.
Branchport - v. in t. of Jerusalem, Yates Co., NY
Bridgewater - v. in Onedia Co., NY
Brockport - v, in t. of Sweden, Monroe Co., NY
Brooklyn - c. in Kings Co., NY
Brownville - t. and v. in Jefferson Co., NY
Brutus - t. in Cayuga Co., NY
Buffalo - c. in Erie Co., NY
Butternuts - t. in Otsego Co., NY
Cambridge - t. and v. in Washington Co., NY
Camden - v. in Oneida Co., NY
Camillus - t. and v. in Onondaga Co. NY
Canajorhie - v. and t. in Montgomery Co., NY
Canandaigua - t. and v. in Ontario Co., NY
Canasarega - l. in t. of Sullivan, Madison Co., NY
Canastota - v. in Madison Co., NY
Cardiff - v. in t. of LaFayette, Onondaga Co. NY
Cato - t. and v. in Cayuga Co., NY
Catskill - t. and v. in Greene Co., NY
Caughnewaga - old Dutch settlement at site of now Fonda, Montgomery Co., NY
Cayuga - v. in t. of Aurelius, Cayuga Co., NY
Cayuga Bridge - bridge in above town
Cazenovia - t. and v. in Madison Co., NY
Center Lisle - early p.o. in t. of Lisle, Broome Co., NY
Central Square - v. in t. of Hastings, Oswego Co., NY
Chatham - t. and v. in Columbia Co., NY
Cherry Valley - v. and ck. in t. of same name, Otsego Co., NY
Chittenango - v. in t. of Sullivan, Madison Co. NY
Cicero - t. and v. in Onondaga Co., NY
Clarkson - t. and v. in Monroe Co., NY

Clay - t. and v. in Onondaga Co., NY
Clinton - v. in Oneida Co., NY
Clintonville - v. in t. of Au Sable, Clinton Co., NY
Clyde - v. in Wayne Co., NY
Collamer - h. in t. of DeWitt, Onondaga Co., NY
Columbia - t. and v. in Herkimer Co., NY
Conquest - t. and s. in Cayuga Co., NY
Constantia - v. and t. in Oswego Co. NY
Corning - c. in co. of same name, NY
Cortland - c. in co. of same name, NY
Cumberland - name of some two dozen + v., c., cos. in the USA,
    Canada, etc., also a co. in England.
Delhi - t. and v. in Delaware Co., NY
Delphi - v. in t. of Pompey, Onondaga Co., NY
DeWitt - t. and v. in Onondago Co., NY
Eagle Village - s. west of v. of Manlius, in t. of same name, Onondaga
    Co., NY
Eaton - t. and v. in Madison Co., NY
East Bloomfield - t. and v. in Ontario Co., NY
East Cayuga - s. in t. of Aurelius, Cayuga Co., NY
East Hampton, L. I. - t. and v. in Suffolk Co., NY
Elbridge - v. and t. in Onondaga Co., NY
Evans Mills - v. in t. of LeRay, Jefferson co., NY
Fabius - t. and v. in Onondaga Co., NY
Fairfield - t. and v. in Herkimer Co., NY
Fairmount - v. in t. of Camillus, Onondaga Co., NY
Farmersville - v., also called, "Farmers", in t. of Covert, Seneca Co., NY
Fayetteville - v. in t. of Manlius, Onondaga Co., NY
Fenner - s. in t. of same name, Madison Co., NY
Fleming - v. and t. in Cayuga Co., NY
Florence - t. and v. in Oneida Co., NY
Floyd - t. and v. in Oneida Co., NY
Fulton - c. in Oswego Co, NY
Geddes - t. and v. in Onondaga Co., NY
Geneseo - t. and v. in Livingston Co., NY
Geneva - c. in Ontario Co., NY
Genoa - t. and v. in Cayuga Co., NY
Glen Haven - l. in t. of Sempronius, Cayuga Co., NY
Gloversville - v. in t. of Johnstown, Fulton Co., NY
Granby - t. in Oswego Co., NY
Groton - t. and v. in Tompkins Co., NY
Hamilton - t. and v. in Madison Co., NY
Hannibal - t. and v. in Oswego Co., NY
Hartsville - h. in t. of Manlius, Onondaga Co., NY
Hastings - t. and v. in Oswego Co., NY
Havana - v. in t. of Catharines, Schuyler Co., NY
High Bridge - l. ca 4 mi. west of Manlius village where bridge crosses
    over Limestone Ck., t. of Manlius, Onondaga Co., NY
Homer - v. and t. in Cortland Co., NY

Howlett Hill - former p. o. in t. of Onondaga, Onondaga Co., NY
Ira - t. and v. in Cayuga Co., NY (sometimes called Ira Hill or Ira Center)
Ithaca - c. in Tompkins Co., NY
Jacksonville - one of a number of l., v., etc. in Onondaga, Westchester, Tompkins, Otsego, and Greene Cos., NY
Jamestown, c. in t. of Ellicott, Chautauqua Co., NY
Jamesville - v. in t. of DeWitt, Onondaga Co., NY
Jefferson - v. in Greene Co., also Schoharie Co., NY; also a co. in NY
Jeromesville - not located. Possibly a l. in t. of Pompey, Onondaga Co., NY
Johnstown - t. and v. in Fulton Co., NY
Jordan - v. in t. of Onondaga Co., NY
Kirkville - v. in t. of Manlius, Onondaga Co., NY
LaFayette - v. in t. of LaFayette, Onondaga Co., NY
Lansing - t. in Tompkins Co., NY
Lansingburgh - t. and v. in Renesselaer Co., NY
Laurenburgh Co., NC
Ledyard - t. in Cayuga Co., NY
Lenox - t. and l. in Madison Co., NY
LeRoy - t. and v. in Genesee Co., NY
Lima - v. and t. in Livingston Co., NY
Little Falls - t. and v. in Herkimer Co., NY
Little Utica - h. in t. of Lysander, Onondaga Co., NY.
Lisle - v. and t. in Broome Co., NY
Liverpool - v. in t. of Salina, Onondaga Co., NY
Lockport - t. and v. in Niagara Co., NY
Lodi - t. and v. in Seneca Co., NY
Lyons - t. and v. in Wayne Co., NY
Lysander - t. in Onondaga Co., NY
McLean - v. in t. of Groton, Tompkins Co., NY
Macedon - v. and t. in Wayne Co., NY
Madison - t. and v. in Madison Co., NY
Manchester - t. and v. in Ontario Co., NY
Mandana - v. and t. of Skanealetes, Onondaga Co., NY
Manlius - v. and t. in Onondaga Co., NY
Manlius Center - former v. on old Erie Canal, between Fayetteville and Minoa, t. of Manlius, Onondaga Co., NY
Marathon - v. and t. in Cortland Co., NY; also v. in t. of Flushing, Queens Co., NY
Marblehead - v. in Essex Co., MA, also Ottawa Co., IL
Marcellus - v. and t. in Onondaga Co., NY
Marcellus Falls - v. in Onondaga Co., NY
Marietta - v. in t. of Marcellus, Onondaga Co., NY
Matthew's Mills - h. (N. Manlius p.o.) in t. of Manlius, Onondaga Co., NY
Messina Springs - l. in t. of DeWitt, Onondaga co. NY
Mentz - t. in Cayuga co., NY
New Baltimore - v. and t. in Greene Co., NY

New Woodstock - v. in t. of Cazenovia, Madison Co., NY
Mexico - t. and v. in Oswego Co., NY
Middlefield - t. in Otsego Co., NY
Middleville - v. in t. of Fairfield, Herkimer Co., NY
Milan - l. in t. of Locke, Cayuga Co., NY
Mohawk - v. in t. of German Flats, Herkimer Co., NY
Montezuma - v. and t. in Cayuga Co., NY
Moravia - v. and t. in Cayuga Co., NY
Morrisville - v. in t. of Eaton, Madison co., NY
Mottville - v. in t. of Skaneateles, Onondaga Co., NY
Mount Morris - t. and v. in Livingston Co., NY
Navarino - v. in t. of Onondaga, Onondaga Co., NY
New Hartford - v. in Oneida Co., NY
New Haven - t. and v. in Oswego Co., NY
New York - largest city in NY
New York Mills - t. and v. in Oneida Co., NY
Niagara Falls - t and c. in Niagara Co., NY; site of renowned waterfalls.
Niles - t. in Cayuga Cco., NY
Nine Mile Creek - stream flowing through t. of Camillus, Onondaga Co., NY
Northampton - unable to identify; either England or MA
Norwich - c. and co. seat of Chenango Co., NY
Nunda - t. and v. in Livingston Co., NY
Oaksville - v. in t. of Otsego, Otsego Co., NY
Onondaga - t. in co. of same name, NY
Onondaga (Hill) - v. in t. of Onondaga, Onondaga Co., NY
Onondaga Hollow - l. in t. of Onondaga, Onondaga Co., NY
Onondaga Valley - v. in t. of Onondaga, Onondaga Co., NY
Onondaga West Hill - l. west of Onondaga (Hill) Village
Oran (Oren) - v. in t. of Pompey, Onondaga Co., NY
Oriskany - v. in t. of Whitestown, Oneida Co., NY
Orville - l. in t. of DeWitt, Onondaga Co., NY
Ossian - t. and v. in Livingston Co., NY
Oswego - c. in Co. of same name, NY
Oswego Falls - v. in t. of Granby, Oswego Co., NY; waterfall near Fulton, Oswego co., NY.
Otisco - t. and v. in Onondago Co., NY
Ovid - t. and v. in Seneca co., NY
Owasco - t. and v. in Cayuga Co., NY
Owasco Lake - l. in t. of Fleming, Cayuga Co., NY; also one of Finger Lakes of NY
Palermo - t. and v. in Oswego Co., NY
Palmyra - t. and v. in Wayne Co., NY
Paris - t. in Oneida Co., NY
Penfield - t. and v. in Monroe Co., NY
Penn Yan - v. in t. of Milo, Yates Co., NY
Perryville - v. on border of t. of Fenner & Stockbridge, Madison Co., NY

Pharsalia - t. and v. in Chenango Co., NY
Phelps - t. and v. in Ontario co., NY
Plainville - l. in t. of Lysander, Onondaga Co. NY
Plattsburg - t. and v. in Clinton Co., NY
Polksville - early p. o.. in t. of Lysander, Onondaga Co., NY, now called Little Utica
Pompey - t. and v. Onondaga Co., NY
Pompey Hill - same as Pompey
Pompey Hollow - s in t. of Pompey, Onondaga co., NY.
Port Hollow - not located
Port Byron - v. in t. of Mentz, Cayuga Co., NY
Port Hollow - not located, prob. port on old Erie Canal.
Poughkeepsie - c. and t. in Dutchess Co., NY
Prattsburg - t. and v. in Steuben Co., NY
Preble - t. and v. in Cortland Co., NY
Pulaski - v. in t. of Richalnd, Oswego Co., NY
Richfield - t. and v. in Otsego Co., NY
Richmond - v. in co. of same name; t. in Ontario co., NY
Rochester - c. in Monroe Co., NY
Rome - c. in Oneida Co., NY
Romulus - t. and v. in Seneca Co., NY
Rushville - v. in t. of Potter, Yates Co., NY
St. Croix - (in this instance) is. in Caribbean Ocean
Sackets Harbor - v. in t. of Hounsfield, Jefferson Co., NY
Salem - t. and v. in Washington Co., NY also s. in t. of Portland, Chautauqua co., NY
Salina - former t. and v. in Onondaga Co., NY now encompassed by c. of Syracuse
Saratoga - v. and t. in co. of same name, NY
Saratoga Springs - t. in Saratoga Co., NY
Schenectady - c. in co. of same name, NY
Scipio - t. and v. in Cayuga Co., NY
Schaghticoke - t. in Rensselaer Co., NY
Schroeppel - t. in Oswego Co., NY
Schuylerville - t. and v. in Westchester Co., NY
Scriba - t. in Oswego Co., NY
Scott - v. in t. of same name, Cortland Co., NY
Sempronius - t. in Cayuga Co., NY
Sennett - v. and t. in Cayuga Co., NY
Seneca Falls - t. and v. in Seneca Co., NY
Sherburne - t. and v. in Chenango Co., NY
Skaneateles - v. and t. in Onondaga Co., NY
Smithfield - t. and v. in Madison Co., NY
Sodus - t. and v. in Wayne Co., NY
South Bay - v. in t. of Ft. Ann, Washington Co., NY; also one of several water inlets.
South Cortland - v. in t. of Cortlandville, Cortland Co., NY
South Marcellus - l. in t. of Marcellus, Onondaga Co., NY
South Onondaga - v. in t. of Onondaga, Onondaga Co., NY

Spafford - t. and v. in Onondaga Co., NY
Springport - t. in Cayuga Co., NY
Sterling - t. in v. in Cayuga Co., NY
Sullivan - s. in t. of same name in Madison Co., NY
Summer Hill - v. and t. in Cayuga Co., NY
Syracuse - c. in Onondaga Co., NY
Throopsville - v. in t. of Throop. Cayuga Co., NY
Trenton - t. and v. in Oneida Co., NY
Troy - c. in Rensselaer Co., NY
Truxton - v. and t. in Cortland Co., NY
Tully - t. and v. in Onondaga Co., NY
Union Springs - v. in t. of Springport, Cayuga Co. NY
Utica - c. in Oneida Co., NY
VanBuren - t. and v. in Onondaga Co., NY
VanBuren Center - l. in t. of VanBuren, Onondaga Co., NY
Venice - v. and t. in Cayuga Co., NY
Vernon - t. and v. in Oneida Co., NY
Verona - t. and v. in Oneida Co., NY
Vesper - v. in town of Tully, Onondaga Co., NY
Vienna - t. and v. in Oneida Co., NY
Virgil - v. and t. in Cortland Co., NY
Volney - t. and v. in Oswego Co., NY
Warners - v. in t. of VanBuren, Onondaga Co., NY
Washington - v. in t. of same name, Dutchess Co., NY
Watertown - c. and t. in Jefferson Co., NY
Waterloo - t. and v. in Seneca Co., NY
Watervale - v. in t. of Pompey, Onondaga Co., NY
Weedsport - v. in t. of Brutus, Cayuga Co., NY
West Dryden - v. in t. of Dryden, Tompkins Co., NY
Westfield - t. and v. in Chautauqua Co., NY
Western - t. in Oneida Co., NY
Westhampton - v. in t. of Southampton, Suffolk Co., NY
Whiteboro - v. in t. of Whitestown, Oneida Co., NY
Whitestown - t. and v. in Oneida Co., NY
Wolcott - v. and t. in Wayne Co., NY
Woodstock - sometimes used for New Woodstock, v. in t. of Cazenovia, Madison Co., NY
Woodstock - v. and t. in Ulster Co., NY
Worcester, t. and v. in Otsego Co., NY

Abbey, Joseph, of Syracuse and Rebecca Mead of Syracuse, m. at Onondaga, 15 Dec. 1831. SC

Abbey, William Jr., and Sophronia Fuller in Onondaga 31 Dec. 1829. OR 6 Jan. 1830

Abbot, Abijah, druggist of Syracuse and Mary A. Webb m. in Pompey 25 Jan. 1830. OR 27 Jan. 1830

Abbott, William, of Clinton, and Lucretia Green of Clay, m. 20 Oct. 1830. OR 27 Oct. 1830

Abell, Capt. Edward, of New York and Helen E. Clift, dau. of William Clift of Skaneateles, m. at Skaneateles 17 July 1856. SD

Abraham, Joseph, of Troy and Loretta Potter of Spafford, m. at Syracuse, NY 4 July 1850. SD

Ackely, Isaac, of CT and Rebecca Cone, m. 1 Oct 1833. STJ

Adams, Abial, and Amanda Webster, dau. of Ephraim Webster, m. at Onondaga 21 Mar. 1819. OR

Adams. Alanson, of Amber, m. Lucinda A. Griffin of Amber, 21 May 1840. SC

Adams, Elijah, m. Patty Oliver at Preble (18 Oct.) 1817. OR

Adams, Rev. O., of Evans Mills and Phebe Ann Calkins of Marcellus, m. at Marcellus 6 Oct. 1842. SC

Adams, Squire, and Ruthala Carpenter m. at Manlius, 22 Feb. 1828. SA

Agan P. H., of the Onondaga Standard, and Hannah E. Stevens, dau. of Hon. John L. Stevens, m. at Cicero 16 Oct. 1847. SC

Aiken, Edward, and Mrs. Elpha R. Bradley both of Marcellus, m. at Marcellus 28 Oct. 1841. SC

Aiken, Edward L., of Michigan and Harriet M. Sandford of Summer Hill, m. at Summer Hill 2 Sept. 1841. SC

Ainslie, Andrew and Diademia Dennigan m. Nov. 1815. OR

Ainslie, John and Margaret Morton, m. at Manlius -- Apr. 1826. OR

Aldrich, Jasper, of Skaneateles and Louisa Armstrong of Skaneateles m. at Marcellus 26 Oct. 1852. SD, 1852

Allen, Chauncey W. of Schuylerville and Mrs. E. J. Snyder of Marcellus m. 4 May 1847. SC

Allen, D. Ezekiel of Constantia and Ellen Lynch of Cicero, m. at Cicero (19 June) 1823. OR

Allen, Franklin of Delphi and Lucy Hart, dau. of Samuel Hart, m. at Pompey Center (20 Jan) 1847. OD

Allen, Isaac M. of the Cayuga Patriot and Susan Mott of Skaneateles, m. at Skaneateles 17 Aug. 1831 OR 31 Aug. (1831)

Allen, Jacob H., of Borodino and Ann Jennett, dau. of the late Jonathan Wyckoff. m. at Skaneateles 24 May 1848. SD

Allen, Jared and Mrs. Jane Fuller, m. at Onondaga, -- -- 1815. OR

Allen, John and Hannah, dau. of William Hempsted of Pompey, m. at Fayetteville (9 June) 1847 OD

Allen, Joseph A., principal of the Syracuse Academy and Lucy T., dau. of Aaron Burt, m. 24 Nov. 1845. SC

Allen, Lemuel, of Scipio and Eliza Oakley of Skaneateles, m. 14 Mar 1832. STJ

Allen, Michael, of PA, and Electa Steele of Auburn, m. 1 Oct. 1839. SC

Allis, Caleb Wells, of Skaneateles, and Latitia, dau. of Valentine Willetts of Skaneateles, m. 15 July 1840. SC

Almy, Hiram and Rebecca, dau. of Elisha Crosby, m. at Cortland 15 Aug. 1838. SC

Alvord, Thomas G. and Charlotte C. Earll, m. at Syracuse, 15 Apr. 1851. SD

Ames, Dr. Calvin, of Lysander and Tryphena Hatch of Columbia, m. at Columbia Herkimer Co. -- Dec. 1816. OR

Ames, Marcus, of Marshfield, MA and Jane A. Vanderburgh of Syracuse, m. at Syracuse 15 Oct. 1853. SD

Amidon, Almer, of Skaneateles and Sarah Ann Parker of Skaneateles m. 23 Oct. 1834. SC

Amidon, David, of Navarino and Rhoda Hall of Navarino m. there -- Jan. 1842. SC

Amidon, Miles, and Martha Cleveland m. at Skaneateles 19 Mar. 1835. SC

Amidon, Moses P., and Sophia Starr m. in Onondaga 3 Jan. 1830. OR 13 Jan. 1830

Anderson, Jonathan of Pompey m. Clarissa Leach of Cicero, at Cicero 18 Feb. 1829. SG&A

Anderson, Samuel and Charlotte Ann Fulton, both of Auburn, m. at Skaneateles 22 May 1849. SD

Anderson, Thomas B., of Spafford and Caroline Crout, m. 1 Dec. 1836. SC

Anderson, William of Skaneateles and Mary Ann Ferguson of Auburn, m. at Skaneateles 17 Jan. 1846. SC

Andrews, Benjamin, and Louisa Palmer, both of Liverpool m. at Syracuse 7 Aug. 1834. SG

Andrews, Cyrus, and Harriet Gaylord m. 1 Jan. 1832. STJ

Andrews, William, Jr., and Violet Andrews, m. at Homer. (17 May) 1820. OR

Annis, C. L., of Salina, and Minerva P. Wismore of Syracuse, m. at Syracuse (6 Jan.) 1847. OD

Anthony, Daniel P., and Ruhama A. Terry of Scott, NY, m. 9 May 1852. SD

Appleton, Rev. Samuel and Sarah Ann, dau. of the late Sylvester Gardner m. at Manlius 30 Sept. 1839. SC

Archibald, Samuel of Oswego and Adeline Mason of Sempronius, m. at Sempronius 23 Feb. 1838. SC

Arnold, David H., of Homer and Julia Randall of Cortland, m. at Cortland, 29 Oct. 1853. SD

Arnold, James T., of OH and Susan T. Carrington, of Marcellus, m. at Marcellus, 13 Aug. 1834. SC

Atwater, Thomas J., and Cordelia Van Schaick both of Sempronius, m. 4 July 1850. SC

Atwater, Zenas of Onondaga and Mary Burt, m. at Johnstown, (21 May) 1817. OR

Atwell, George H. and Orange S. Tillotson [sic] both of Cazenovia, m. at Syracuse (13 Jan.) 1847. OD

Atwill, Winthrop, editor of the Oswego Daily Journal and Emily J. Pardee of Oswego, m. 12 June 1851. SD

Austin, Alanson, of Skaneateles and Marian Brinckerhoff of Marcellus, m. at Marcellus 29 Dec. 1841. SC

Austin, Alvah, of Sempronius and Frances Taylor of Moravia, m. at Moravia, 5 July 1834. SC

Austin, George, of Skaneateles and Almira C. Morrison of Oswego, m. at Oswego 9 June 1852. SD

Austin, Kellogg, of Skaneateles and Sarah Miller of Lyons, m. 29 Dec. 1853. SD

Averill, Lyman R., of Salina and Hannah Smith of South Bay, m. 7 Jan. 1824. OG

Avery, Allen H., of Manlius and Abigail G., dau. of Daniel Platt of Skaneateles, m. 28 Mar. 1848. SC

Avery, Cyrus, and Lurinda Jones, m. in Pompey 3 Feb. 1831. OR 16 Feb. [1831]

Avery, Edgar, of Ledyard and Eliza K., dau. of Rev. J. Worthing of Amber, m. at Amber (26 Jan.) 1847. OD and SC

Avery Samuel, and Lucinda Jones m. in Pompey, 3 Feb. 1831. OR 16 Feb. [1831].

Ayres, George, of CT and Esther Norman of Orville, m. 14 Oct. 1831. OR 2 Nov. [1831].

B

Babcock, Dr. P., of Lyons, NY and Lucena, dau. of M. Chase of Onondaga Hill, m. 2 Sept. 1849. SD

Babcock, Worden, and Melvina Copp, dau. of Thomas Copp, m. at Spafford, 15 Nov. 1836. SC

Babcock, Worden, of Chautauqua Co. and Caroline Almy of Spafford, m. at Spafford, 14 Oct. 1841. SC

Backus, Charles, of Groton and Lovina Carruth of Preble, m. at Preble, 16 June 1846. SD

Bacon, Hiram, of Skaneateles and Charlotte Dean of Owasco, m. at Skaneateles 28 Oct. 1834. SC. Also STJ

Badger, Newton, of Bridgewater and Mrs. Eliza Kennet Kinne, late of DeWitt, m. at Sherburne (3 Mar.) 1847. OD

Badman, Mr., of Auburn and Jane Rhoades of Skaneateles, m. at Skaneateles, 18 Aug. 1850. SD

Bagley, George W., of Skaneateles and Rebecca W. Sherman of Sennett, m. at Sennett, 12 Oct. 1848. SD

Bailey, ----, of Otisco and Charlotte Tinkham of Spafford, m. at Auburn, 30 June 1852. SD
Bailey, Benjamin F., of MI and Florilla Bailey of Elbridge, m. at Elbridge, 18 Jan. 1853. SD
Bailey, Bradie, and Amy Winchell, m. at Tully, (7 Jan.) 1819. OR
Bailey, George, and Olive Madison, m. at Fabius, (27 Apr.) 1826. OR
Bailey, Gordon, of Otisco and Louisa Smith of Spafford, m. at Preble, 27 Aug. 1845. SC
Bailey, John, of Syracuse, and Mary Ann Hyde of Salina, m. at Salina, 14 June 1825. SG
Baker, Asa, and Hannah Robinson, m. in Lysander (7 Jan.) 1819. OR
Baker, Asa, of Marcellus and Huldah Hancock, of Barre, MA, m. at Marcellus 17 Mar. 1842. SC
Baker, Ashbel S., and Norissa Wethey, both of Borodino, m. at Auburn, 6 Oct. 1848. SD
Baker, Benjamin R., and Thirza L. Griffin, both of Marcellus, m. there, (27 Oct.) 1846. OD
Baker, Charles L., of Syracuse and Maria Wood of Salina m. in Salina, 18 Oct. 1827. SA
Baker, E. P., of Otisco and Elizabeth Austin of Skaneateles, m. at Skaneateles, 27 Sept. 1842. SC
Baker, Edward, of Penn Yan and Maria S. Wheeler of Auburn, m. at Auburn, 21 Apr. 1839. SC
Baker, Erastus, Jr., merchant of Jordan, and Rhoda Staring m. in Herkimer, (3 Feb.) 1830. OR
Baker, George C. W., of Owasco and Hannah Cuddeback of Skaneateles, m. 20 Oct. 1852. SD
Baker, Dr. Isaac, of Navarino and Sarah M. Bedell, dau. of Lewis (?) Bedell of Otisco, m. 5 June 1845. SC
Baker, James, of Navarino and Susan Barber of Marcellus, m. in Borodino, 2 June 1842. SC
Baker, John D., and Elizabeth Cole, m. at Skaneateles, 1 Dec. 1838. SC
Baker, John F., and Helen M. dau. of P. N. Rust of Syracuse m. at Utica, 26 May 1844. SC
Baker, Joseph, and Sarah Binning of Sennett (?) m. at Skaneateles, 21 July 1850. SD
Baker, Leonidas L., and Nancy A. Emmons, both of Tully, m. at Tully, 23 Aug 184? (1842-45) SC
Baker, Lewis E., and Harriet Bedell m. at South Onondaga, 7 Aug. 1853. SC
Baker, Roland S., and Sarah E. Rockwell, both of Marcellus, m. at South Onondaga, 21 Feb. 1853. SD
Baker, Samuel, and Philena Haskill, m. at Pompey 21 Sept. 1819. OR
Baker, Smith, of Saratoga, and Sarah A. Cramer of LaFayette, m. at LaFayette, 6 Dec. 1853. SD
Baker, Zebulon, and Sally Ann Taft, m. at Spafford, 6 Mar. 1836. SC
Balch, David, and Polly, dau. of Jude Comstock, m. at Onondaga, 20 Jan. 1831. OR 26 Jan. [1831]

Baldwin, Alvin, of Scriba and Matilda Haskins of Phoenix, m. at Scriba, (25 Dec.) 1846. OD
Baldwin, Daniel, of Geddes and Caroline David, m. in Jordan (23 Feb.) 1831. OR
Baldwin, Daniel, of PA and Cornelia DeVoe, dau. of Elijah DeVoe of Owasco, m. in Owasco, 25 Oct. 1835. SC
Baldwin, Harvey, of Onondaga and Laura, dau. of Hon. James Geddes, m. at Onondaga, 16 Nov. 1824. SG, OR
Baldwin, Harvey, of Ira and Sarah Shumway of Owasco, m. at Owasco 6 June 1852. SD
Baldwin, John Cornelius, and Calista Wilcox, m. at Oran (?), (15 Nov.) 1818. OR
Ball, Ashley H., of Rochester, and Frances Fidelia, dau. of Samuel Ball of Marcellus, m. 15 May 1844. SC
Ball, Samuel, merchant of Marcellus and Orpha Whitney of Marcellus, m. at Marcellus, 8 June 1852. SD
Bangs, Francis H., of Amber, and Sarah Carrington of Marcellus, m. at Marcellus, 21 Oct. 1834. SC
Banker, John H., of Schenectady, and Jane Wilcox of Auburn, m. at Auburn, 14 Sept. 1839. SC
Barber, Alonzo W., of Skaneateles and Lydia Owen of Marcellus, m. at Marcellus, 11 Jan. 1844. SC
Barber, C. Eugene, and Cornelia L., eldest dau. of Hon. Christopher Morgan, all of Auburn, m. at Auburn 4 Oct. 1853. SD
Barber, Dr. Chauncey, and Danny Duel, m. in Onondaga, (13 July) 1831. SG&GA
Barber, David, and Harriet, dau. of Moses H. Hinsdale of Pompey, m. 6 Oct. 1828. SG&GA
Barber, Henry, and Irene West, both of Scott, m. at Scott, 20 Jan. 1853. SD
Barber, Joel, and Rachel Baker, both of Marcellus, m. at Marcellus, 27 July 1840. SC
Bardite(?), Nathan T., of MI and Almira Jane Treat of Mentz, m. at Skaneateles, 9 Oct. 1838. SC
Barker, William, and Betsey Ann Knapp of Spafford, m. 10 Jan. 1844. SC
Barlow, Rev. William, of Ontario Co., and Sally J. Canfield of Pompey, m. at Pompey, -- Sept. 1816. OR (Note: Rev. Mr. Barlow was at St. Paul's Church, Syracuse, 1826-1828.)
Barnes, Allen, of Syracuse, and Mary E. Strobeck of Whitesboro, m. at Whitesboro, (7 Dec.) 1846. OD
Barnes, Asa, of WI, late of Pompey, and Ann S., dau. of David H. Leonard of DeWitt, m. at DeWitt, (3 Mar.) 1847. OD
Barnes, H. N., of Syracuse and Helen Seely, m. in Cazenovia 16 May 1837. SW
Barnes, Horace, and Phoebe Higgins, m. at VanBuren Centre (1 July) 1846. OD
Barnes, Ira, and Tryphena Elsworth, m. at Camillus, 4 Aug. 1827. SA

Barnes, James E., of Camillus and Alicia Brown of Marcellus Falls, m. at Marcellus Falls 16 Feb. 1851. SD

Barnes, William, and Elizabeth Ann Thompson of Syracuse, m. (30 Apr.) 1845. SD

Barnes, William, and Elizabeth Ann Thompson of Syracuse, m. (31 May) 1845. SC

Barnum, Lucius, and Annis Jones, m. at Onondaga 30 Apr. 1823. OG, OR

Barnum, Marcus, and Elizabeth Lownsbury (Lawnsbury), m. in LaFayette, (19 Jan. 1830 or 1831. OR

Barnum, Martin, and Augusta P. June, m. at Manlius, 21 July 1852. SD

Barnum, Thomas E., editor of the Syracuse Advertiser, and Clarissa Atwater of Canandaigua, m. at Canandaigua, 21 Sept. 1826. SA

Barrett, William, and Patty Morey, m. at Pompey, (5?) Mar. 1818. OR

Barrett, Zena, of Preble and Mary Wilcox of Tully, m. at Cortland, (23 Sept.) 1846. OD

Barrow, Henry D., of Wisconsin and Mary M. Bennett of Auburn, m. 18 June 1852. SD

Barthelomew, Rev. Orlo, and Julia Ann Peck, dau. of N. Peck, m. at Skaneateles, 15 Nov. 1836. SC

Bascom, Ansel B., son of Silas Bascom, b. at Skaneateles 1 Jan. 1802; admitted to the Onondaga Bar 1826; went to Seneca Falls and d. there 30 Aug. 1862; m. 6 Sept. 1827 Eliza Sherwood, dau. of Isaac. See Bascom Genealogy.

Bascom, Ansel, of Seneca Falls, m. Elizabeth Sherwood, dau. of Isaac Sherwood, at Skaneateles, (11 Sept.) 1827. SA

Bascom, Silas, b. Southampton, MA 29 June 1772; m. 19 Apr. 1801, Betsey Hatch (b. 5 Dec. 1881 (ed. note: should be 1781?), d. 2 Nov. 1822). He settled in Skaneateles and d. there 5 Apr. 1826. See Bascom Genealogy.

Bates, Abner, and Electa Edwards, dau of the late Simeon Edwards of Skaneateles, m. at Skaneateles, 2 Aug. 1837. SC

Bates, George W., of Vernon, NY and Harriet H. Gilbert of Hannibal, NY m. at Marcellus, 14 May 1850. SD

Bates, James, and Amanda Yarrington, m. at Syracuse 23 Dec. 1828. SG&GA

Bates, Joseph, and Mary Ann Eaton m. at Eaton 8 Mar. 1831. OR

Bates, Larkin, and Liana Brooks, m. at Manlius, -- Jan. 1826. OR

Beach, John and Mrs. Sarah J. Ellis, both of Baldwinsville, m. at Baldwinsville, 30 Mar. 1850. SD

Beach, John C. and Elizabeth Townsend Porter, dau. of the late James Porter of Skaneateles, m. at New York City, 10 July 1851. SD

Beach, John M., of Fabius and Amanda Pease m. at Pompey, 20 Jan. 1831. OR 16 Feb.[1831]

Beach, Orlando, and Julia Herring both of Marcellus, m. 4 Mar. 1835. SC

Beach, William, and Laura Crandall, m. at Salina, -- June 1816. OR

Beach, Col. William, of SC and Mary Elizabeth Hess, late of Syracuse, m. at Brooklyn 9 Apr. 1851. SD

Beagle, William, of Cicero and Susan Robinson, m. in Clay 29 Nov. 1829. OR 16 Dec. [1829]

Bean, George F., and Mary A. Montague both of Fulton m. at Syracuse, (30 May) 1847. OD

Bean, J. H., of Syracuse and P. B. Hough, m. at Manlius 20 July 1852. SD

Beard, E. H., and Helen C., dau of Hon. Manoah Pratt, all of Pompey, m. there, 20 Oct. 1852. SD

Beardsley, James, and Charlotte A. Hopkins, dau. of Col. Hezekiah Hopkins, m. at Pompey, 1 May 1828. SG&GA

Beardsley, W. C., and Catherine Richardson, dau. of Hon. J. L. Richardson, m. at Auburn 17 Apr. 1838. SC

Beardsley, Wetmore, of Batavia and Diana Veeder of Otisco, m. at Otisco, 3 Oct. 1840. SC

Beattie, Thomas, and Eliza Peckham, both of Syracuse, m. at Cazenovia 25 July 1830. OR 28 July [1830]

Becker, David, and Eunice A. Legg dau. of William Legg, all of Borodino, m. 7 July 1851. SD

Becker, Henry, of Clay, ae 80, and Esther Rhodes of Schroeppel, ae 74, m. in Schroeppel -- Dec. 1849. SD

Beebe, William L., merchant of Skaneateles, and Mary Douglass, dau. of Archibald Douglass, m. at Skaneateles 7 Feb. 1827. SA

Beecher, Hiram S., and Elsie Curtis, m. at Salina 18 Oct. 1827. SA

Beecher, R. Malcom, of Port Byron, and Malvina E. Cuddeback, dau. of J. C. Cuddeback, m. at Syracuse, 16 Mar. 1853. SD

Belden, Friend, and ---- VanBenthuysen, both of Amber, m. (16 Mar.) 1825. OR

Belden, Merrett, and Mary Ann Scoville m. at Salina, 25 Feb. 1829. SG&GA

Belden, Roswell, and Lucinda Hale, m. 27 Sept. 1835. STJ

Belding, Dexter, and Miss ---- Wilson of Orville, m. at Orville, 8 Feb. 1850. OR 10 Feb. [1850]

Belote, John, and Amanda Wilcox, m. at Onondaga Valley -- Apr. 1816. OR

Benedict, Mr., of Scipio, and Mrs. Ann Nichols of Onondaga Valley, m. at Onondaga Valley, (28 Oct) 1822. OR

Benedict, Anson W., and Harriet R. Allen, dau. of Aaron Allen, m. at Skaneateles, 8 Oct. 1846. SD

Benedict, Bradley, late of Onondaga Valley and Narcissa Cook of Cayuga, m. at Cayuga, (22 Dec.) 1822. OR

Benedict, Harmon B., and Caroline A. Hall, dau. of Ralph Hall of Skaneateles, m. 27 Nov. 1851. SD

Benedict, Harmon B., and Charity Litherland, adopted dau. of Samuel and Rebecca Litherland of Skaneateles, m. 21 Apr. 1842. SC

Benedict, Isaac A., and Martha A. Crandall, m. at Skaneateles, 29 Sept. 1838. SC

Benedict, James, and Maria Worden, m. at Auburn, 13 Mar. 1838. SC

Benedict, Melvin, and Mariette Randall, m. 24 Mar. 1834. STJ
Benedict, Noah P., of Syracuse and Sarah Kellog of Skaneateles, m. at Lodi, 13 Mar. 1847. SD
Benedict, Sidney L., of Skaneateles and M. Orinda Baker, dau. of Brayton Baker of Marcellus, m. at Marcellus, 11 June 1851. SD
Benham, Hon. Miles, of Penn Yan and Mrs. Cynthia Munroe of Elbridge, m. at East Cayuga, 3 Sept. 1843. SC
Benjamin George, and Julia Haskins both of Fabius m. at Skaneateles, 3 July 1845. SC
Bennett, Cephas, of Utica and Stella Kneeland, dau. of Amasa Kneeland, m. at Marcellus, 10 Jan. 1827. SA
Bennett, John, of Port Byron and Ann M. More of Skaneateles, m. at Skaneateles, 4 July 1853. SD
Bennett, Miles W., of Camillus and Harriet Jerome of Onondaga, m. 14 Feb. 1824. OG
Bennett, Thomas, and Mrs. Elizabeth Burt, late of Springfield, MA, m. at Syracuse, 7 Feb. 1828. SA
Benning, Jeremiah, and Ann Maria Eggleston, m. 21 Jan. 1839. STJ
Benson, Capt. Abijah, of Otisco and Mrs. Freelove Smith of Spafford, m. at Skaneateles, 25 Aug. 1836. SC
Benson, Frederick, of Jordan and Frances, dau. of Erastus Baker, m. in LaFayette, 19 July 1831. OR
Bentley, Daniel and Evalina Buck, m. at Marcellus (21 Mar.) 1819. OR
Bentley, George A., and Electa M. Gaylord, m. at Skaneateles, 15 Nov. 1848. SD
Bentley, Russell, and Julia Betts, m. at Warners, 10 Oct 1824. SG
Bentliff, James, and Harriet Snook, dau. of John Snook of Skaneateles, m. (29) Sept. 1847. SD
Benton, William, Jr., of Skaneateles and Mary Peck of Spafford, m. at Marcellus 3 Nov. 1840. SC
Bernard, Hiram G. and Louisa Topham, m. at Salina 7 Feb. 1829. SG&GA
Berry, Sidney, of Sennett, and Nancy A. Stebbins of Spafford, m. at Spafford 31 Dec. 1843. SC
Best, Henry, of Bristol, Eng. and Harriet Brown of Syracuse, m. at Syracuse (Thanksgiving Day) 1841. SC
Bevier, Abraham, and Mrs. Marty Martz DeHart, m. at Owasco, 6 June 1841. SC
Bevier, Matthew N., and Sarah M. Dennis m. at Ira, NY, 3 June 1837. SC
Bickford, Dearborn B., and Anne Gates, m. at Manlius, -- Nov. 1815. OR
Bidlack, John, and Almira West, both of Sennett, m. at Camillus 20 Jan. 1828. SA
Bigelow, Hiram, of Baldwinsville, and Maria Tarbox, m. at Baldwinsville, 24 Apr. 1825. SG

Bigelow, Thomas O., and Mary Bolles, m. at Baldwinsville, 29 Mar. 1852. [No reference given]

Billings, Daniel L., of Homer and Almira Dickenson, m. at Syracuse, 7 Dec. 1831. OR 14 Dec. [1831]

Billings, Henry C.,and Eliza Terwilliger both of Skaneateles, m. at Skaneateles, 12 June 1850. SD

Billings, Richard, and Huldah Keller, both of Skaneateles, m. at Syracuse, 2 Jan. 1847. SC

Bingham, A. C., and Delia Tomkins, m. at Camillus, 5 Apr. 1850. SD

Bingham, John, and Lucy Gage, m. (6 Jan.) 1819. OR

Bird, Ira W., and Christine L. Stoner, m. at Skaneateles, 24 Sept. 1851. SD

Bird, Truman E., of Skaneateles and Ellen M. Higley, dau. of Homer Higley, m. at Plainville, OH, 8 Sept. 1852. SD

Bird, William, and Lucretia Stanton, m. at Syracuse, 15 Nov. 1829. OR 25 Nov. [1829]

Birdsall, Daniel, of Macedon, and Maria Dorland of Skaneateles, m. -- Sept. 1839. SC

Birdseye, Victory J., of Pompey, and Betsey Ann Marsh of Pompey, m. 14 Oct. 1840. SC

Birdsley, Abram, and Susan Chandler, m. 2 May 1839. STJ

Bisdee, Samuel, of Baldwinsville, and Margaret Cuddeback of Skaneateles, m. 14 Apr. 1842. SC

Bisdee, Sidney, and Mary Taylor, dau. of Lewis Parker, m. at Skaneateles, 1 Nov. 1843. SC

Bishop, Col. Ira, and Sarah Hutchinson, both of Marcellus, m. 10 May 1842. SC

Bishop, William, and Almira Wiborn, both of Manlius, m. at Manlius, 27 Jan. 1830. OR 10 Feb. [1830]

Blackman, Alpheus, and Mary Ann Slocum, m. at Syracuse -- Oct. 1827. SA

Blake, Isaac, of Ira, and Angeline Southard of Ira, m. at Plainville, 23 Feb. 1853. SD

Blakesley, A. J., of Jordan, and P. J. Stockwell of Auburn, m. at Auburn, 30 Oct. 1842. SC

Blakesley, Horace, of Syracuse, and Sarah Sackett of Auburn, m. at Marcellus 24 Oct. 1824. SG

Blanchard, Thomas, of DeWitt, and Clarissa Sweeting, m. at Clinton, NY, 19 Jan. 1841. SC

Blanchard, Williard, and Caroline Goddard, both of Manlius, m. in Marcellus, 10 Mar. 1831. OR 30 Mar. [1831]

Bliss, Elijah W., and Orphena Kind, m. at Onondaga Hollow (17 Nov.) 1818. OR

Bodine, Gilbert, and Hannah Selover of Owasco, m. 2 Feb. 1841. SC

Boley, John, of VanBuren, and Sally M. Roe of Lysander, m. at Lysander, 24 Nov. 1853. SD

Booth, Rev. Robert R., of Troy, and Emma L. Lathrop, dau. of Rev. R. E. Lathrop of Auburn, m. 26 Oct. 1853. SD

Booth, Spencer, of Branchport, and Mrs. Sophia Hopkins of Mar[cellus?], m. 7 Nov. 1843 (or 1837). SC

Bosworth, John, of Ossian, NY and Fidelia M. Recard of Homer, m. at Skaneateles, 4 Mar. 1847. SD

Boutwell, Harvey, and Hannah Paddock of Salina, m. 3 Aug. 1823. OG

Bow, Titus, and Mrs. Sally Scoville, m. at Van Buren, (1 Mar.) 1848. OD

Bowe, Benjamin, of Providence, RI, and Mary, dau. of Horace Butts of Syracuse, m. at DeWitt 10 Oct. 1853. SD

Bowen, Spencer, of Sennett, and Sarah Myrick, m. in Elbridge 3 Dec. 1839. OR 6 Jan. 1830

Brackett, Edward H., of Fulton, and Mary A. Crane of Salina, m. at Salina, 3 May 1838 (or May 31). SC

Brackett, Rueben, and Caroline Wheeler both of Camillus, m. at Camillus (12 Apr.) 1825. OR

Bradford, Gabriel, and Olive Mary Curtis, dau. of John Curtis, m. at Skaneateles 15 Sept. 1847. SC

Bradford, Thomas, and Abby Parsons, both of Skaneateles, m. 15 Sept. 1847. SC

Bradley, Daniel, of the firm of C. & D. Bradley, and Sarah Gilbert, m. in Groton, NY, -- Nov. 1829. OR 25 Nov. [1829]

Bradley, F. H., of Millpoint, C.[anada] W.[est] and Margaret D. Robinson, dau. of Dr. H. Robinson, m. at Auburn, 8 June 1853. SD

Bradley, Isaac, of Marcellus and Mary B. Thompson, dau. of Peter Thompson of Skaneateles, m. at Skaneateles 1 Feb. 1842. SC

Bradway, Hiram, P. M., (Presbyterian Minister?) of Fulton, and Esther A. Phillips, dau. of Elijah Phillips of Granby, m. at Granby, (28 Dec.) 1847. OD

Brainard, John Osborne, of Skaneateles, and Christina J. Depew, dau. of John Depew, m. at Poughkeepsie, 4 Dec. 1845. SC

Brainard, Samuel S., of New York, and Pamela DeCost, dau. of Capt. DeCost of Skaneateles, m. at Skaneateles, 19 July 1832. SC. See also Brainard Genealogy.

Branch, John, and Cynthia Grove, (or Greaves) m. 9 Sept. 1837. STJ

Brand, Ross, and Elizabeth Vosseller, m. 30 Dec. 1827. SA

Breed, Barnet M., of Manlius and Diadama Hatch, m. in Pompey, 3 Jan. 1831. OR 19 Jan [1831]

Breed, George, of Phoenix, and Mary Sweet, dau. of Charles W. Sweet of Clay, m. at Clay (4 Feb.) 1847. OD

Breed, Henry G., and Abigail N. Root, both of Jordan, m. at Jordan, 3 May 1853. SD

Brewster, Dr., of Mexico, and Julia Clark, dau. of Dr. Deodatus Clark, m. at Scriba, Oswego Co., -- Oct. 1822. OR

Brewster, Dr. Henry E., of Truxton and Ruth Merrill, m. at Fabius, -- June 1826. OR

Brewster, Isaac W., and Belinda Bylington [sic] m. at Jamesville, (17 Oct.) 1822. OR

Briggs, Frederick, and Julia M. Earll, dau of Hezikiah Earll, all of Skaneateles, m. at Brockport 27 Feb. 1850. SD

Briggs, George, of Marcellus, and Susan Cooper of Amber, m. at Amber, 11 Jan. 1842. SC

Briggs, H. F., of Marietta and Mayette, dau. of George Spalding of Borodino, m. 12 Sept. 1844. SC

Briggs, Isaac, and Electa Edwards, dau. of Alanson Edwards, m. at Skaneateles (15 Feb.) 1820. OR

Briggs, Dr. Lansing, and Angelica Worden, m. at Auburn, 14 Aug. 1838. SC

Briggs, Hon. Russell, of MI, and Jane, dau. of Archibald Douglass, m. at Skaneateles, 11 Oct. 1843. SC

Briggs, Samuel, and Ann Willsey of Marcellus, m. at Onondaga South Hill, (13 Feb.) 1820. OR

Briggs, Samuel G., of Skaneateles and Ann Cogswell of Auburn, m. at Auburn, 28 Sept. 1842. SC

Briggs, William S., of Skaneateles and Maria A. Merritt of Venice, m. at Venice, NY 3 June 1840. SC

Brigham, Charles P., of Auburn and Luraina M. Burdick of OH, m. at Auburn, 2 Sept. 1849. SD

Brinkerhoff, A. L., of Onondaga and L. A. Welch of Marcellus, m. 5 Nov. 1845. SC

Brinkerhoff, Stephen, of New York and Mrs. Mary Yates of Chittenango, m. in New York City, (14 Sept.) 1848. OD

Britnall, Hiram, and Cynthia Pratt, m. at Syracuse, 17 Feb. 1842. SC

Bristol, John, and Salome Culver of Auburn, m. 19 Aug. 1851. SD

Bristol, William, and Mehitable Case, both of Utica, m. at Utica, -- Nov. 1824. OR

Brokaw, Newton, and Dorinska Forbush, both of Niles, m. 27 Dec. 1852. SD

Bronson, Henry C., of Utica and Eliza M., dau. of Carperat [sic] of Auburn, m. at Auburn 8 Sept. 1845. SD (?)

Bronson, LaFayette, and Emily Rice, both of Manlius, m. at Manlius (27 Jan.) 1847. OD

Brooks, Daniel, of Lysander, and Rosanna Finch of Syracuse, m. in Syracuse, 24 Dec. 1830. OR

Brooks, Edward, and Roana Humphrey, both of Auburn, m. 11 Aug. 1852. SD

Brower, Abraham, of Truxton, and Ruth Merrill, m. at Fabius, -- June 1826. OR

Brown, Austin, and Calaphonia Morgan, both of Scott, m. at Homer, 25 June 1856. SD

Brown. Bela, and Elizabeth Cushman, both of Salina, m. 19 May 1830. OR, 25 May [1830]

Brown, Charles, and Helen N. White, dau. of J. C. B. White, all of Marcellus, m. at Marcellus, 21 Aug. 1843. SC

Brown, Emanuel, of Coburg, Canada, and Mary Ann Thorn, of Syracuse, m. at Syracuse, (30 Nov.) 1846. OD

Brown, Harmon G., of Owasco, and Harriet VanBlaricum, of Conquest, m. at Conquest, 23 Sept. 1852. SD

Brown, Harvey, of Orleans Co., and Genet P. Ford, of Skaneateles, m. at Syracuse, 15 Feb. 1849. SD

Brown, Joshua W., of New York, and Sarah E., dau. of Russell Frost of Skaneateles, m. at Skaneateles, 18 Nov. 1843. S?

Brown, Truman, and Abigail Moon, both of Spafford, m. at Spafford, 5 July 1845. SC

Brown, William, and Ann Warner, both of Lima, m. in Onondaga, 3 Oct. 1831. OR, 5 Oct. [1841]

Bruce, R. A., of New York, and Mary M. Beebe, late of Auburn, m. at Ravenswood, L. I. (Long Island), 17 Nov. 1853. SD

Bryan, Dr. Orlando M., of IL, and Jane L. Voorhees, dau. of Col. J. E. Voorhees, m. at Baldwinsville, 26 June 1849. SD

Bryant, J. W., of Fulton, and Mary D., dau. of W. H. Knowlton, of Jordan, m. at Jordan, 26 June 1844. SC

Bryant, Samuel C., and Phebe North, both of Syracuse, m. at Syracuse, 15 Mar. 1825. SG

Bryant, Samuel S., and Mrs. Betsey Mack, both of Syracuse, m. at Syracuse, 1 Feb. 1830. OR 10 Feb. [1830]

Buck, Elisha P., and Caroline Phillips, of Marcellus, m. at Marcellus, 5 Dec. 1838. SC

Buel, Achilles, and Elizabeth Parkhurst, m. at Fairfield, (7 June) 1820. OR

Buel, Simon, of Lysander, and Julia, dau. of the late Jonathan Wycoff, of Skaneateles, m. 15 Oct. 1851, in Skaneateles. SD

Buel, Walter, of Skaneateles, and Miss Welch, of Amber, m. at Amder, 17 June 1835. SC

Buffington, Charles B., of Cataraugus Co., and Adeline Hager, of Spafford, m. 22 Sept. 1840. SC

Bullock, Addison, of Skaneateles, and Maria Toles, of Auburn, m. at Auburn, 11 May 1853. SD

Burch, William, of Homer, and Lottie F. Sherman, of Summer Hill, m. at Summer Hill, 17 Feb. 1879. SD

Burdick, Benjamin, and Margaret Yordon, both of Hastings, m. at Syracuse, 1 Jan. 1852. SD

Burdick, F. J., and Adeline T., dau. of B. F. Comstock, of Union Springs, m. 10 Jan. 1853. SD

Burdick, Solomon, and Sophia Hall, m. at Spafford, 15 Mar. 1835. SC

Burge, William T., of Canada, and Harriet Lee, of Skaneateles, m. at Skaneateles, 26 Feb. 1835. SC

Burgess, Jeremiah, of Granby, and Lydia Brainard, of Elbridge, m. at Elbridge, 6 July, 1842. SC

Burke, William O., and Phebe Yates, m. at Skaneateles, 1 Jan. 1839. SC

Burlington, B. H., and Elizabeth Converse, m. at Manlius, 4 Sept. 1839. SC

Burnet, Moses D., and Mrs. Helen Creed, widow of John B. Creed, m. at Syracuse, -- July 1826. OR

Burnet, Charles J., Jr., and Eliza DeCost, of Skaneateles, m. 1 Oct. 1840. SC
Burnett, Galusha, late of Skaneateles, and Margaret Sherwood, both of Nunda, m. 27 Apr. 1847. SC
Burnett, James A., of Constantia, and Mrs. M. L. Rand (or Randolph) of Skaneateles, m. at Skaneateles, 5 Mar. 1851. SD
Burnett, R. M., and Frances M. Edwards, m. at Skaneateles, 11 July 1849. SC
Burns, Peter, and Elizabeth, dau. of Joshua Bates, late of Skaneateles, m. at Syracuse, 9 May 1850. SD
Burr, William S., of Richmond, VA, and Laura P. Sanford, dau. of the Late Judge Sanford, of Skaneateles, m. at Geneva, 7 Dec. 1853. SD
Burridge, John Jr., and Elizabeth Cuddeback, both of Skaneateles, m. at Skaneateles, 4 Sept. 1851. SD
Burrill, Nathan, of Jordan, and Mary Dilts, of Skaneateles, m. 4 June 1851. SC
Burroughs, Jeremiah, of Skaneateles, and Sophronia Eaton, of Spafford (?), m. at Spafford, 22 Sept. 1840. SC
Burroughs, Smith, and Mary Goodell, of Otisco, m. 15 Jan. 1845. SC
Burt, Oliver T., and Rebecca Johnson, m. at Syracuse, 12 Jan. 1848. OD
Burt, Walter, of Lysander, and Eleanor Fort, of Scaghticoke, m. at Syracuse, (13 Jan.) 1847. OD
Bush, Silas, Jr., and Hannah F. Rhoades, of Skaneateles, m. 3 June 1835. SC
Bushnell, Dr. A. L., of Cincinnati, OH, and Mary E., dau. of Cyrus Rhodes, of Skaneateles, m. 3 June 1835. SD
Bussey, Oren E., and Caroline Frink, both of Baldwinsville, m. at Baldwinsville, 2 Oct. 1843. SC
Butler, Levi, and Ann Sunderland, (or Sutherland), m. at Pompey, (6 July) 1826. OR
Butler, Linus, of Onondaga, and Polly Landon of Salina, m. in Salina, -- Dec. 1815. OR
Butler, Martin S., of Skaneateles, and G. Holley, of Brookfield, CT, m. at Brookfield, CT, 28 Aug. 1852. SD
Butler, Samuel, and Harriet Hall, m. in Onondaga, (19 Jan.) 1831. OR

C

Cadwell, John, and Mary E. Porter, both of Onondaga, m. in Onondaga 14 Jan. 1830. OR 20 Jan. [1830]
Cadwell, S. W., and Mrs. Sarah Norton, both of Syracuse, m. at Syracuse 27 May 1840. SC
Cadwell, Stephen, and Alina Adams, m. at Onondaga Hollow, (23 Nov) 1817. OR
Cady, A. Stoyell, of Moravia and Mary Abigail Parsons, dau. of Rev. Levi Parsons, of Marcellus, m. 25 July 1843. SC

Cady, Platt, of New York and Esther M. Richards of Mottville, m. at Marcellus, 3 Aug. 1851. SD

Cane, Lyman, and Jane Clark, both of Elbridge, m. at Skaneateles, 13 Feb. 1851.

Callendar, Richard, and Mary A. Hicks, both of Marietta, m. at Marietta 16 Dec. 1851. SD

Cameron, Alexander, of Pompey and Mrs. Fuller of Buffalo, m. in Buffalo 5 Feb. 1830.

Campbell, B. S., printer of Syracuse, and Mary L. Wilkinson, m. at Messina Springs, 15 May 1851. SD

Campbell, George, and Lucinda Russell, m. in Onondaga (27 Apr) 1831. OR

Canfield, Clement G., and Elizabeth Belieu, m. in Jordan 6 Apr. 1830. OR, 14 Apr.[1830]

Caple, Edmund, of England, and Eliza Haurl, of Skaneateles, m. 15 Oct. 1846. SC

Carberry, John P., and Mary Ann Ward, both of Auburn, m. at Auburn, 4 Feb. 1827. AFP

Carpenter, Benjamin, of Saratoga Co., and Maria Irwin, of Skaneateles, m. at Skaneateles, 6 Mar. 1839. SC

Carpenter, Samuel S., and Prudence G. Comins, m. in Tully 24 Feb. 1831. OR 2 Mar. [1831]

Carpenter, William N., of Detroit, and Amanda Gibbs, of Skaneateles, m. 26 Aug. 1845. SC

Carr, Moses, of Skaneateles, and Emeline P. Gray, of Wolcott, NY, m. at Wolcott, NY, 2 May 1852. SD

Carson, James and Mary Orr, both of Jordan, m. at Skaneateles 14 July 1853. SD

Cary, Albert, late of Skaneateles, and Mary J. Bradley, of Oxford, m. at Norwich, 30 Apr. 1849. SD

Cary, Bradley, of Syracuse, and Matilda Phelps, of Lodi, m. in Lodi, 30 Dec. 1830. OR 5 Jan. [1830].

Case, John, of Howlett Hill, and Miriam S. Bacon, of Mandana, m. at Mandana, 1 Oct. 1845. SC

Case, Lewis, of Otisco, and Mary Jane Turbish, of Spafford, m. at Amber, 21 May 1842. SC

Case, Miles, and Betsey Marks, m. 23 Sept. 1819 [Thurs. eve. last]. OR 29 Sept. [1819]

Case, William of Gloversville, and Mary, dau. of John Mathews, of Elbridge, m. at Liverpool, (18 Nov.) 1846. OD

Castle, Benjamin and Wealthy, dau. of William Smith, m. at Cicero, 12 Oct. 1828. SG&GA

Catton, James, of Skaneateles, and Rhoda Skeels, of Marcellus, m. at Marcellus, 8 Apr. 1840. SC

Catton, John W., and Amelia Robinson, of Marcellus Falls, m. 18 Mar. 1844. SC

Catton, Stanford C., and Jane Ellen Terry, of Onondaga Hill, m. 19 Nov. 1839. SC

Center, Lyman, and Julia Chittenden, of Jordan, m. at Syracuse, 5 Nov. 1845. SC

Chadwick, Holland W., of Brockport, NY, and Matilda, dau. of Hezekiah Earll, m. by Rev. Algernon G. (?) Hollister, at Skaneateles, 6 July 1829. ST

Chafee, Joseph, of Marcellus, and Phebe Enos, of Spafford, m. at Otisco, 13 Mar. 1836. SC

Chafee, Walter, of Marcellus, and Mary, dau. of Horace Davis, of Otisco, m. at Otisco, 16 Oct. 1846. SC

Cháffee, Ariel C., and Delia Ann Whiting, of Marcellus, m. 31 Dec. 1840. SC

Chamberlain, Joshua, of Clay, and Percy Kendall of Geddes, m. -- May 1849. SD

Champlin, C. H., of Marcellus and Caroline Bessey, of Camillus, m. at Camillus, (23 Oct.) 1825. OR

Chaplin, Gen. William L., and Theodosia Gilbert, m. at Glen Haven, 12 Aug. 1851. SC

Chapman, Dr. Chandler, of Onondaga, and Eugenia Pease, dau. of James Pease, m. at Syracuse, 1 June 1837. SW

Chapman, Edward, of Syracuse, and Florilla Parsons of the same place, m. at Syracuse, 3 Oct. 1824. SG

Chapman, Fredus T., and Mrs. Lucretia Willington, both of Marcellus, m. at Skaneateles, 26 Oct. 1841. SC

Chapman, Lincoln and Sarah Reed, m. at Marcellus, 1 Jan. 1828. SA

Chappell, Augustus and Harriet Wicks, m. at Pompey, (7 Jan.) 1819. OR

Chappell. Newton, and Harriet C. Backus, both of Auburn, m. there 12 June 1853. SD

Chase, David, and Lucinda Hall, of Skaneateles, m. 8 Jan. 1845. SC

Chase, James, and Ann Pulsifer, both of Cato, m. at Liverpool (4 July) 1846. OD

Chase, Wesley, and Susan Beebe, m. at Onondaga Hill, 4 Oct. 1839. SC

Chaney, Lucius, of Syracuse and Sarah Bicknell, of Morrisville, m. at Morrisville 25 Oct. 1826. SA

Child, William H., of the Skaneateles Telegraph, and Susan Hill, m. in Waterloo, 7 Dec. 1829. OR 16 Dec. [1829]

Childs, Philander and Mary Ann Preston, dau. of Deacon Preston, m. at Clay (10 Dec.) 1828. OR

Christler, David and Amy Wiltsie, m. in Marcellus (27 July) 1831. OR

Church, Darius D., and Jane, dau. of Jacob Cuddeback, m. at Skaneateles, 24 June 1828. SC

Church, George, and Nancy Pickle, both of Manlius, m. in Lodi, 1 Mar. 1831. OR 9 Mar. [1831]

Church, Joseph M., of Skaneateles, and Maria Louise Goddwin (Goodwin?), of Providence, RI, m. 10 Aug. 1841. SC

Church, William, and Chloe Page, both of Cicero, m. at Marcellus, 30 July 1840. SC

Churchill, Henry, and Jane Littlefield, both of Skaneateles, m. at Skaneateles, 21 July 1850. SD
Clapp, Chester, and Sally Hillman, m. at Pompey, (5 Mar) 1818. OR
Clapp, Morris H., of Pompey, and Deborah A. Smith, of DeWitt, m. at DeWitt, (19 Jan) 1848. OD
Clark, C. C., and Catharine McCormick, both of Syracuse, m. at Syracuse, 15 Jan. 1853. SD
Clark, Charles P., late of Skaneateles, and Aurelia L. Nolton [sic], dau. of R. W. Knowlton, of Syracuse, m. at Syracuse, 18 Oct. 1849. SD
Clark, Daniel, and Nancy Wattles, m. at Manlius , -- Sept. 1816. OR
Clark, Edward, of Troy and Harriet M., dau. of Chauncey Betts, of Lysander, m. at Lysander, (27 Jan.) 1847. OD
Clark, Edward, of Skaneateles, and Louisa Forncrook, of Elbridge, m. at Elbridge, 4 Jan. 1841. SC
Clark, Edwin, of Skaneateles, and Esther W. Parsons, of Northampton, m. 14 Oct. 1852. SC
Clark, Gerard, and Adreste (or Areste) Chittenden, both of Jordan, m. in Skaneateles, 2 June 1848. SD
Clark, Horace, and Mariette, dau. of Norman Watson, m. at Skaneateles, 11 May 1841. SC
Clark, Horatio Nelson and Eliza Bailey, m. at Geddes village (31 Oct.) 1832. OR
Clark, Isaiah, and Olive Kinney, m. at Pompey (7 Jan.) 1819 . OR
Clark, Jesse, and Elizabeth Wood, both of Syracuse, m. at Syracuse, 22 June 1850. SD
Clark, John S., of Auburn, and Angeline Martin of Fleming, m. at Auburn, 13 Nov. 1853. SD
Clark, Julius, editor of the Syracuse Argus, and Cornelia Morse m. at Syracuse, 15 Dec. 1831. SC
Clark, Luther, of New Haven, and Mrs. John Pain of Scriba, m. at Scriba, 11 Apr. 1831. OR 11 May [1831]
Clark, Noah, and Julia Palmer, m. at Auburn, 16 Oct. 1845. SC
Clark, Philetus and Elvira Parent, both of Otisco, m. at Otisco, 15 Sept. 1835. SC
Clark, Selah and Nancy McDonald, m. at Otisco, (15 Dec.) 1819. OR
Clark, William of Fabius, and Sally Wadsworth of Onondaga, m. at Onondaga Hollow, -- Dec. 1817. OR
Clark, William E., of Skaneateles, and Maria A., dau. of Benoni Smith, of Scipio, m. at Scipio, 8 May 1845. SC
Clarke, Hiram, of Mentz, and Louisa Mills, of Montezuma, m. at Auburn, 27 Sept. 1853. SD
Clatworthy, John, and Harriet Harle, both of Skaneateles, m. at Auburn, 25 Dec. 1844. SC
Clatworthy, William, and Desire L., dau. of Benjamin Springer, all of Skaneateles, m. 7 June 1843. SC
Clements, Elihu, and Samantha Reed, both of Pompey, m. at LaFayette, 16 Jan. 1829. SG&GA

Clements, J. M., of Amber, and Elizabeth Wiltsie, of South Marcellus, m. 8 Nov 1853 SD

Cleveland, Lewis W., of Skaneateles, and Mrs. Amelia Warner, of Williamsburg, MA, m. at Williamsburg, 13 Oct. 1840. SC

Clift, Hiram, and Polly Knapp, of Marcellus, m. at Homer, 22 May 1843. SC

Clift, Myron, of Skaneateles and Elizabeth Hutchinson, m. at Onondaga, 18 Feb. 1846. SC

Clift, Wills and Esther Ann Hoyt, of Sennett, m. 1 Oct. 1844. SC

Clitson, Henry, and Miss --- Naracong, both of Skaneateles, m. at Skaneateles, 25 Dec. 1845. SC

Clough, Daniel O.,and Susan M. Keeney, both of Fabius, m. at Fabius, 2 Sept. 1849. SD

Clough, Henry and Ellen Blackhurst, both of Auburn, m. at Auburn, 4 July 1850. SD

Clute, Isaac of Auburn and Emeline DeLine of Aurelius, m. at Elbridge, 12 Aug. 1838. SC

Cobb, Alford, and Mary M., dau. of D. B. Bickford, m. at Syracuse, 13 May 1852. SD

Cobb, Rev. Daniel, of Elbridge, and Mary Earll, of Marcellus, m. at Marcellus 13 Feb. 1844. SC

Cobb, Ira H., and Esther Bates, late of Skaneateles, m. at Syracuse, 9 May 1850. SD

Cobb, Rufus, of Auburn and Adelaide Waiser, 3 Mar. 1833. STJ

Codington, George, of Seneca Falls, and Minerva R. Pease, of Spafford, m. at Spafford, 23 June 1835. SC

Coffin, Charles, and Hannah Ann, dau. of Col. Samuel How, all of Vienna, NY, m. 10 Oct. 1842(?). SC

Colanbrauer, Roman, and Catharine Sampman, late of Germany, m. at Syracuse 9 Sept. 1851. SD

Cole, Dr. Daniel W., of Oswego, and Philura, dau. of the late William Bostwick, m. at St. Peter's Church, Auburn, 25 Dec. 1826. AFP

Cole, Isaac P., and Huldah, dau. of Rev. John Frashur, all of Syracuse, m. at Syracuse, (13 Oct.) 1846. OD

Cole, Jeremiah, and Mahaly Hanchest, m. at Pompey (7 Jan) 1819. OR

Cole, Josiah, and May Jane Sutphen, both of Auburn, m. at Auburn, 5 May 1849. SD

Cole, Samuel D., of Owasco, and Emma Ford, of Auburn, m. at Auburn, 17 Mar. 1853 SD

Collins, Alonzo, and Mary Jane Rouse, both of Syracuse, m. at Syracuse, 16 Mar. 1852. SD

Colton, Frederick, of Greenbush, and Mary A. Heath of Pompey, m. 18 Aug. 1853. SD

Colvin, Benjamin F., of Syracuse, and Florence, dau. of Alfred Hovey, of Montezuma, m. 9 Apr. 1818. SA

Colvin, Dr. David S., of Syracuse and Nancy Earll, m. at Skaneateles (15 Dec.) 1819. OR

Colvin, David S. of Syracuse, and Harriet E., dau. of Peter B. Morgan, m. 31 Dec. 1827. SA

Comstock, David A., of New York and Maria, dau. of D. Kellogg, of Skaneateles, m. at Skaneateles, 18 Nov. 1834. SC

Concklin, Henry, Jr., of Onondaga and Laura A. Todd, of Manlius, m. 20 Oct. 1853. SD

Congdon, Benjamin F., of Marcellus, and Caroline Bishop, of Otisco, m. in Otisco, (19 Jan.) 1831. OR

Conger, Jacob, of Milan, and Maria Johnson, of Scipio, m. at Scipio 1 Feb. 1827. AFP

Conklin, Newell and Genet Price, m. at Owasco, 8 Sept. 1841. SC

Conklin, William, of Niles, and Maria, dau. of the Hon. John I. Brinkerhoff, m. at Owasco, 9 Feb. 1852. SD

Connor, James, and Sophronia Thomas, both of Skaneateles, m. at Auburn 7 Mar. 1841. SC

Conover, Mortimer, of Skaneateles, and Eugenia Curtis, of Marcellus. m. at Marcellus 28 Oct. 1852. SD

Conover, William H. and Cornelia H. (or R.) Caldwell, of Weedsport, m. at Weedsport, 8 Apr. 1847. SD

Converse, Rev. Augustus L., of Troy, and Mary Ann, dau. of Daniel Kellogg, of Skaneateles, m. (-- May) 1825. OR

Converse, George, of Onondaga, and Mrs. Rebecca Stolp, of Marcellus, m. at Marcellus, 19 Dec. 1840. SC

Cook, Charles, and Mrs. Olive Taylor, both of Syracuse, m. 20 Dec. 1827. SA

Cook, Corydon, of Skaneateles, and Mary Roudley, of the same place, m. 13 Nov. 1850. SC

Cook, Francis, and Celina Dodge, m. -- Nov. 1815. OR

Cook, Henry, and Caroline Hervey, m. at Marcellus, 4 Nov. 1843. SC

Cook, James, and Alminta Newton, m. at Marcellus, 7 Oct, 1831. STJ

Cook, Jonathan, of Marcellus, and Barbara Eldridge, of Niles, m. at Marcellus, 3 Feb. 1850. SD

Cook, Milo, of Mottville, and June Schuff, of Manchester, NY, m. at Manchester, 25 Mar. 1853. SD

Cook, Rev. R. S., and Ann Maria, dau. of Rev. Dr. Mills, m. at Auburn, 1 Nov. 1836. SC

Cook, Rev. R. S., of New York, and Harriet N. Rand, of Pompey, m. by the bride's father, 22 Jan. 1841. SC

Cook, W. H. Of Jordan, and Lydia Arnold, of Elbridge, m. at Elbridge, 26 June 1851. SD

Cook, William, of Camillus, and Harriet, dau. of Gen. Ellis, of Onondaga, m. -- Oct. 1816. OR

Cooley, Rev. E. U., of LaSalle, IL and Sarah A. Adams of the Onondaga Seminary, m. 19 Nov. 1851. SD

Coome, Robert, and Maria Westlake, both of Owasco, m. at Owasco, 3 Oct. 1840. SC

Coon, Cyrus, of Skaneateles, and Lovina Eggleston, of Onondaga Hollow, dau. of John B. Eggleston, m. at Onondaga Hollow, 22 Dec. 1836. SC

Coon, George, of Camillus, and Olive Turner of Skaneateles, m. at Elbridge, 20 Dec. 1843. SC
Coon, J. V. R., and Mrs Clarina (Clarissa?) Weaver, both of Cicero, m. at Skaneateles, 21 Apr. 1840. SC
Coon, Thomas, and Nancy Fidelia Clark, m. at Skaneateles, 21 Dec. 1845. SC
Coon, Thomas, and Cordelia Pollock, m. at Skaneateles 8 Jan. 1839. SC
Coon, William, and Catherine, dau. of Benjamin Eggleston, m. at Skaneateles, 14 Feb. 1839. SC
Coon, William of Geneva, and Amanda Parker, of Skaneateles, m. at Skaneateles 28 Sept. 1843. SC
Coonley, B. and Emily, dau. of C. R. Merriam, m. at Elbridge, 23 Apr. 1838. SC
Corley, Thomas, and Elizabeth Smith, m. 13 Oct. 1836. STJ
Cornell, Abraham, and Betsey Cornell (?), m. at Camillus, 22 Nov. 1824. SG
Cornell, David, and Harriet Elsbury, at Skaneateles, 29 Aug. 1847. SD
Cornell, Elijah B., and Betsey Ann Burdick, m. at Manlius, 15 Dec. 1831. SC
Cornell, Horace and Amy Greenfield, both of Skaneateles, m. 15 Feb. 1844. SC
Cornell, P. D., and Lydia Ann Kelderhouse, m. at Auburn, 26 Feb. 1838. SC
Cornell, William and Mehitabel Ann Smith, both of Camillus, m. at Camillus, 24 Jan. 1828. SA
Corning, Rev. Richard S., of Otisco, and Ann, dau. of the late John Spencer, m. at Albany, -- Jan. 1825. OR
Corning, Rev. Richard S., of Ohio, and Ann, dau. of the late John Spencer, of Albany, m. at Albany, -- Jan. 1825. SG
Cossitt, Rufus, of Onondaga, and Miss ---- Van Kleek, of Poughkeepsie, m. at Poughkeepsie. -- Jan. 1823. OR
Cotton (or Catton), John W., and Amelia Robinson, of Marcellus Falls, m. 18 Mar. 1844. SC
Covil, Elisha, and Lovina Copp, m. at Marcellus, -- Jan. 1818. OR
Covil, Hiram, of Onondaga, and Amanda Loomis, of Marcellus, m. at Marcellus, 27 Nov. 1845. SC
Cowles, Aaron, and Sally Whitmore, of Otisco, m. at Otisco, (16 Dec.) 1824. OR
Cowles, Caleb, of Marcellus, and Hannah, dau. of Chauncey Gaylord, of Otisco, m. at Otisco, (9 Mar.) 1828. OR
Cowles, Francis A., of Cortland, and Sarah C. Dills, of Sennett, m. at Skaneateles, 27 Oct. 1842. SC
Cox, C. E., and Charlotte Harvey, both of Lysander, m. at Lysander, 15 Feb. 1853. SD
Cox, Dr. George, of West Dryden, and Angeline Ricer, of Marcellus. m. at Marcellus, 29 Sept. 1846. SD

Cox, Rev. Samuel H., and Eliza, dau. of Hon. Alfred Conkling, of Auburn, m. 10 Apr. 1845. SC
Coye, David, and Nancy Canfield, m. at Homer, (24 May) 1820. OR
Cramer, Eliphalet, and Electa Fay, m. 19 Sept. 1839. STJ
Cramer, Elifalet [Eliphalet], of WI, and Electa Fay, of Skaneateles, m. at Skaneateles, (20 Sept.) 1839. SC
Cramer, Jacob, and Harriet Harvey both of Ira, m. at Polkville (Little Utica) (17 Jan.) 1848. OD
Crandall, Truman R., of Delphi, and Elizabeth Tabor, of Woodstock, NY, m. at Woodstock, 14 Sept. 1853. SD (New Woodstock?) SD
Crane, John R., and Delia F., dau. of Thomas Wheeler of Salina, m. 9 Dec. 1839. SC
Cravath, Obed, and Hannah Cushing, m. at Homer, (29 Mar.) 1815. OR
Crawford, William, and Abigail Marsh, m. 25 Jan. 1837. SJC
Creed, John B. and Helen Pellse, m. at Onondaga Hollow, -- Oct. 1816. OR
Crego, Stephen, and Laura Green, m. at Onondaga, (9 Apr.) 1826. OR
Cribb, William, and Susan Shepard, m. at Onondaga Hollow, -- Nov. 1817. OR
Crippen, Darius, m. Sybil E. Richmond (b. VT, Dec. 1797, d. at Brady, MI, 1853). See Richmond Family.
Crofoot, Line, of Preble, and Sarah Elizabeth Fish, m. 17 Sept. 1839. SJC
Cromwell, A. E., of Havana, NY and Caroline Louise, dau. of the late Dr. Hopkins, m. at Skaneateles, 7 Oct. 1841. SC
Cropsey, Daniel, and Maranda Bennett, m. at Syracuse, 15 June 1828. SG&GA
Cropsey, John G., of Sullivan, NY, and Eliza Ann Cropsey (?), of Skaneateles, m. at Skaneateles, 14 Feb. 1842. SC
Crosby, Albert, and Clarissa Dennis, m. in Oran, (2 Feb.) 1831. OR
Cross, Truman, and Emma Legg, m. at Spafford, 14 Mar. 1839. SC
Crossman, John, and Elizabeth Weeks, m. at Skaneateles, 24 July 1852. SC
Crow, Horace, and Asenath Crandall, m. in Fabius, (27 Jan.) 1830. OR
Crowley, Cornelius, of Baldwinsville, and Margaret O'Sullivan, of Marblehead, m. at Salina, 8 Oct. 1851. SD
Crysler, C., of Elbridge, and N. W. Dunbar, of Moravia, m. at Moravia, 19 May 1852. SD
Cuddeback, Cornelius, of Phelps, NY, and Phebe Ann Dotay, of Weedsport, m. at Weedsport, 9 Nov. 1852, both were deaf mutes, graduates of the New York Institute. SD
Cuddeback, David, of Skaneateles, and Fanny W., dau. of George Spaulding, of Borodino, m. 27 Sept. 1843. SC
Cuddeback, LaFayette, of Skaneateles, and Cornelia I., dau. of Munn Davis, m. at Baldwinsville, 5 Jan. 1852. SD

Cuddeback, Simeon, and Ann G. Wyckoff, dau. of Jonathan Wyckoff, m. at Skaneateles, 25 Sept. 1837. SC
Cummings, Albert, of Onondaga and Emily Brown, m. at Otisco, 16 Feb. 1831. OR , 23 Feb. [1831]
Cummings, Ebenezer J., of Syracuse, and Martha B. Ogden of the same place, m. at Syracuse, 4 Aug. 1852. SD
Cunningham, Horace, and Nancy Cook, m. at Syracuse, 17 May 1827. SA
Curry, Francis F., of Utica, and Lucyette, dau. of Ira J. Reynolds, of Syracuse, m. at Syracuse, 13 Sept. 1852. SD
Curtenius, John L., and Mary F., dau. of Judge Young, m. at Whitestown, (14 June) 1820. OR
Curtis, Elijah W., and Amanda, dau. of Erastus Terry, m. in Geddes, 31 Dec. 1829. OR 6 Jan. [1829]
Curtis, Julius, of CT, and Mary Ann Evans, of Spafford, m. at Spafford, 29 June 1834. SC
Curtis, Ralph D. and Alica Ann Wood, m. 10 Oct. 1834. SJC
Curtiss, Fisher, and Susan West., m. in Salina, -- Dec. 1815. OR
Cutter (or Cutler), John R., of Syracuse, and Sarah L., dau. of Robert C. Fulton, of Borodino, m. at Borodino, 18 Oct. 1846. SC
Cuykendall, Archibald, of Onondaga, and Martha Ann Delano, of Skaneateles, m. 29 Feb. 1848. SC
Cuykendall, Benjamin, and Sarah Bacon, of Skaneateles, m. at Skaneateles, 16 May 1839. SC
Cuykendall, William B., merchant, and Adeline Orilda Tompkins, m. at Owasco, 4 Feb. 1852. SD

D

Daggett, Dr. of IL and Clara, dau. of Bishop N. Parsons, of Marcellus, m. 28 Oct. 1845. SC
Dakin, Samuel D., senior editor of the Utica Sentinel and Gazette, and Mary, dau. of Thomas Mumford, of Cayuga, m. at Cayuga, 6 Sept. 1827. SA
Dale, William, and Mrs. Clarissa Seely, m. in Jamesville, (29 Dec.) 1830. OR
Danford, Harvey and Melissa Eno, m. at Clay, 7 Jan. 1829. SG&GA
Daniel, Horace B., of Skaneateles, and Rhoda A. Ward, of Borodino, m. at Borodino, 21 June 1852. SD
Darrow, Addison C., and Sarah H. Cole, both of Niles, m. at Auburn, 1 Mar. 1876. SD
Dart, Benjamin, and Sarah Ingersoll, both of Salina, m. at Cicero, 15 Jan. 1824. OG
Daulton, John W. of Homer, and Sarah C. Strong, of Skaneateles, m. at Skaneateles, 14 Feb. 1853. SD
Davy, John, and Phebe Lee, m. 28 Oct. 1833. STJ

Davey, William H., late of Skaneateles, now of Marysville, MO, and Alva Jane Axtell, of Janesville, IA, m. at Janesville, -- Nov. 1875. SD

Davidson, Kenneth, and Sarah Ann Burnham, m. at Salina, 11 Nov. 1827. SA

Davis, Addison H., of Auburn, and Phebe Ann Shepherd, also of Auburn, m. at Skaneateles, 13 Feb. 1848. SC

Davis, Caleb, and Waty Williams, m. at Onondaga, 5 Jan. 1830. OR

Davis, G. W., and Betsey P. Mead, m. at Marcellus, 11 Oct. 1847. SC

Davis, George T. M., and Susan, dau. of James Webb, all of Syracuse, m. 15 Apr. 1828. SA

Davis, James S., and Ann E. Smith, m. at Syracuse, 29 Aug. 1848. SD

Davis, John, and Laura Henderson, m. in Onondaga, 24 Feb. 1831. OR, 9 Mar. [1831]

Davis, Matthew W., and Margaret, dau. of Joshua Forman, all of Syracuse, m. 31 July 1824. SG

Davis, Richard, and Eliza Blawveat, both of Skaneateles, 5 Sept. 1835. SC

Davis, Ward of Chippewa, Canada West, and Cecilia W., dau. of Henry J. Brower, of Niagara Falls, late of Syracuse, m. at Buffalo, (15 Nov.) 1847. OD

Davison, Abial (Abiel?), and Sophia Miller, m. at LaFayette, Mar. 29 (or Sept.), 1817 (or 1819). OR

Day, Ebenezer W., of MA, and Mary S. Burt, of Otisco, m. at Syracuse, 31 Jan. 1845. SC

Day, Isaac, of Borodino, and Elizabeth Smith, m. 9 June 1836. STJ

Dayton, Nathaniel, of Lockport, and Harriet E. Boies, of Cortland, m. at Cortland, 18 Oct. 1836. SC

Dean, ----, of Mt. Morris, and Mary, dau. of Rev. Joel Bradley, m. at Orville, 14 Sept. 1823. OG

Dean, James C., and Sarah M. Allen, m. at Delphi, 5 June 1849. SD

Dean, Josiah, and Bridget McCan, both of Syracuse, m. at Syracuse, (16 Jan.) 1848. OD

Debua, Henry, and Henrietta Bishop, m. 28 June 1839. STJ

DeCost, Capt. Nash, and Mrs. Hannah Coe, m. 5 Sept. 1839. STJ

Delano, Chauncey B., and Maria Welch, m. at Skaneateles, 23 Dec. 1847. SC

Delano, Elbridge, of Middlefield, NY, and Phebe J. Burton, of Herkimer, m. at Marietta, 27 Dec. 1846. SD

Demon, ----, of Skaneateles, and Julia E. Smith, of Syracuse, m. at Syracuse, 12 Oct. 1848. SD

Denison, Alvin, of Floyd, and Mrs. Deborah B. Wallace, of Skaneateles, m. at South Marcellus, 3 Mar. 1851. SD

Depuy, Philip, and Asenath Howe, both of Owasco, m. at Owasco, 26 Apr. 1846. SD

Derbin, Joseph E., and Mrs. Sarah L. Evans, both of Skaneateles, m. at Auburn, 17 Dec. 1853. SD

Derrick, Simeon, and Hannah Davis, of Skaneateles, m. 13 Apr. 1844. SC

Devoux, Jacob, of Ulster, and Margaret Gumaer, m. at Manlius, (22 July) 1826. OR
DeWater, Joseph, of Sennett, and Mary Jane Taylor, of Elbridge, m. at Skaneateles, 14 Feb. 1849. SD
Dewey, M. L. H., of Sacketts Harbor, and Harriet T. Merriam, of Auburn, m. at Auburn, 29 Dec. 1840 SC
DeWitt, Charles, and Elzina Holden, m. at Skaneateles, 4 Nov. 1838. SC
DeWitt, James, of Marietta, and Charlotte Partidge, of Skaneateles, m. at Skaneateles, 9 Oct. 1844. SC
DeWitt, James, of Niles, and Mary, dau. of Andrew Reed, of Skaneateles, m. at Skaneateles, 7 Oct. 1846. SD
Dexter, David, of Marcellus, and Caroline Cisco, of Brutus, m. at Brutus, 10 June 1824. SG
DeZeng, Rev. Edward, of Skaneateles, and Mary Osborne Russell, dau. of E. A. Russell, of Middletown, CT, m. at Middletown, 21 Sept. 1843. SC
Dibble, Dr. O., and Fannie A. Wheaton, m. at Pompey, 20 Oct. 1875, by Rev. J. Bowman, rector of St. Matthews, [of] Moravia. SD
Dickerson, Job. L., and Lucy Sandford, both of Auburn, m. 10 Dec. 1818. CP
Dickinson, James, and Caroline Frances Knapp, both of Mentz, m. at Skaneateles, 3 Apr. 1850. SD
Dickinson, Pliny, of Syracuse, and Fanny Sackett, dau. of Hon. William A. Sackett, m. at Seneca Falls, 13 Oct. 1852.
Dickinson, Wilmath, and Sarah M. Butin, m. at VanBuren, 24 Dec. 1853. SD
Diltz, Samuel, of Scipio, and Selina Rumsey, of Skaneateles, m. at Fleming, 15 Nov. 1836. SC
Dimon, Henry, late of Skaneateles, and Letitia Merrick, of Auburn, m. at Auburn, 22 May 1853. SD
Dingley, Henry, and Lydia Haines, both of Skaneateles, m. 13 July 1853. SD
Doane, Rev. J., and Maria E. Smith, widow of Hannibal Smith, who was drowned in Owasco Lake 24 June 1837, m. at Mexico, NY, 13 Aug. 1838. SC
Dodge, Harrison B., and Harriet Hannum, both of Skaneateles, m. at Skaneateles, 15 Oct. 1834. SC
Dodge, Harrison B., and Catharine, dau. of Archibald Douglass, of Skaneateles, 7 Feb. 1844. SC
Dole, Capt. Sidney, and Nancy Swan, m. at Salina, (6 Sept.) 1817. OR
Dollen, John, and Emma Strong, both of Skaneatles, m. at Jordan, 4 Apr. 1851. SD
Dolon, Joseph, of Throopsville, and Emeline Benedict, of Auburn, m. at Auburn, 18 Nov. 1853. SD
Donnason, Daniel D., of Hannibal, and Martha Jane Halstead, of Granby, m. at Baldwinsville, 10 Nov. 1853. SD
Dorance, Samuel, and Emily Penny, both of Otisco, m. 8 Sept. 1853. SD

Dorland, James T., of Skaneateles, and Harriet M. Brown, of Bridgewater, NY, m. 30 Sept. 1841. SC

Dorwin, Thomas M., of Vernon, and Waty Adams, of Onondaga Hollow, m. (7 Feb.) OR

Dotay, Isaac, of Sennett, and Emily Davis, of Weedsport, m. at Mottville, 14 Aug. 1853. SD

Doty, Seymour, and Emily Isdell, both of Spafford, m. at Syracuse, 14 Oct. 1852. SD

Douglass, Archibald, and Lydia Peck, m. 25 June 1835. STJ

Douglass, Stephen, of Mrs. Mary Plympton, of Skaneateles, m. 12 Jan. 1843. SC

Douglass, Thomas of Manchester, VT, and Laura G. Clark, of the same place, m. at Manchester, 12 Aug. 1844. SC

Douglass, Thomas, late of Skaneateles, and Julia E. Higby, of Palmyra, m. at Palmyra, 7 June 1847. SD

Dove, James of Skaneateles, and Rebecca Ann Way, of Navarino, m. at Navarino, 1 Dec. 1852. SD

Dow, Daniel C. of Manlius, and Fanny Burnham. m. in Salina, 25 Nov. 1830. OR, 8 Dec. [1830]

Dow, "the celebrated", Lorenzo, and ---- Doalbears, of Montville, m. at Hebron, CT, -- Apr. 1820. OR

Downer, Truman, and Remembrance Nye, of Marcellus, m. 26 Oct. 1828. SA

Downer, William and Isabella Fish, m. at Onondaga Valley, 13 Jan. 1839. SC

Downs, F. B., of Otisco, and C. S. Rouley, dau. of P. C. Rouley, of South Cortland, m. at South Cortland, 19 July 1853. SD

Doxey, Leonard, M., of Auburn, and Huldah A. Beach, of Baldwinsville, m. at Syracuse, 11 Oct. 1853. SD

Doxy, Nathan, and Polly Clarke, both of Skaneateles, m. at Mentz, 21 Dec. 1846. SC

Drake, Charles H. of Jordan, and Betsey C., sister of Francis Baker, and dau. of Erastus Baker, m. in LaFayette, (3 Aug.) 1831. OR

Drake, Samuel of Lockport, and Cornelia H. Benson, of Skaneateles, m. at Skaneateles, 6 Nov. 1837. SC

Drake. Simeon, and Sophronia Cole, m. at Pompey. -- Feb. 1824. OG

Draper, George, and Elizabeth Brown, m. at Syracuse, 8 Sept. 1839. SC

Drew, Joseph, and Mary Wilkie, m. in Belle Isle, 20 Feb. 1831. OR, 23 Feb. [1831]

Duckett, Edward, and Widow Ann Hole, both of Skaneateles, m. 21 Dec. 1844. SC

Duell, R. Holland, of Fabius, and Mary L. Cuyler, of Pompey, m. at Pompey, (10 Sept.) 1846. OD

Duguid, Nelson, and Angeline Woodward, m. in Pompey, (27 Jan.) 1830. OR

Duguid, William, and Eveline VanBuren, m. at Pompey, 14 Dec. 1831. SC

Duncan, Thomas, Capt., U.S.A., and Mary S. Wilson, dau. of Joseph S. Wilson, m. at Washington, DC, 25 Aug. 1852. SD

Dunlap, John A., and Sarah M. Vrooman, m. at Onondaga, 30 June 1852. SD

Dunning W. H., of IA, and Jessie M. Tonkin, of Auburn, m. at Kenosha (WI?), 6 Sept. 1852. SD

Durbin, Edwin, and Mrs. Mary Hydon, m. at Skaneateles, 26 Jan. 1853. SD

Durrant, Samuel and Mrs. Mary Smith, m. at Salina, 14 Jan. 1839. SC

Dwight, Alanson, and Harriet Reynolds, m. at Auburn, 30 May, 1838. SC

Dwinnell, Wright, of Sennett, and Eveline Tiffany, of Pompey, m. at Sennett, 19 Feb. 1839. SC

Dwinelle, J. W., and Cornelia Bradley Stearns, dau. of Dr. J. Stearns, m. at Pompey Hill, 11 Aug. 1841. SC

Dwinelle, Dr. Justin, and Mary Viall (?) (or Viell) dau. of Henry F. King, all of Tully, m. at Tully, (25 May) 1847. OD

Dyer, Dr. Edward G., and Ann Eliza, dau. of William Morse, m. in Trenton, 19 Jan. 1831. OR 2 Feb. [1831]

Dyer, William, of IN, and Diana Downer, of Onondaga, m. at Onondaga, 11 Sept. 1839. SC

E

Eager, of Manlius, and Fanny Ingalls, of Burlington, Otsego Co., NY, m. -- Dec. 1817. OR

Earle, Ward T. and Weltha A. Hardy, both of Homer, m. at Homer 10 July 1856. SD

Earll, Delos, of Skaneateles, and Julia A., dau. of Lucius Mellen, m. at Elbridge, 3 June 1845. SC

Earll, F. C. (or O.), of Salina, and Charlotte C. Merrill, of Cortland, m. at Cortland, 6 Feb. 1844.

Earll, John H., and Elenora, dau. of Daniel Watson, m. at Skaneateles, 26 Jan. 1848. SC

Earll, Julius, of Skaneateles, and Sarah S., dau. of Charles Hill of Auburn, m. at Auburn, 6 Apr. 1852. SD

Earll, Nehemiah H., and Avis Burton, m. at Onondaga, -- Oct. 1816. OR

Earll, Samuel, and Jane Murray, m. at Tully, 29 May 1838. OR

Earll, Sanford, of Skaneateles, and Eunice Hebard, of Homer, m. at Homer 9 July 1834. SC

Earll, Sheppard, of South Marcellus, and Emeline Smith, of Spafford, m. at Spafford, 9 Mar. 1852. SD

Eastman, Bartlett, and Lucy Grover, m. at Pompey, 13 Aug. 1823. OG

Easton, Harry, and Polly Blakesly, both of Onondaga, m. at Salina, 30 Dec. 1823. OG

Eastman, William and Luck Hard, of Cicero, m. at Cicero, (1 Sept.) 1825. OR

Eaton, Daniel, and Susan Fuller, both of Onondaga, m. at Onondaga, 10 Dec. 1823. OG

Eaton, Theodore H., of Buffalo, and Ann Eliza Gibbs, m. 9 Oct. 1839. STJ

Eaton, Thomas H. of Detroit, and Eliza Gibbs, of Skaneateles, 9 Oct. 1839. SC

Eddsen, and Cora Day, both of Cicero, m. at Baldwinsville, 23 Feb. 1853. SD

Edwards, Abner, of IL and Harriet S., dau. of Ralph Hall of Skaneateles, m. at Skaneateles, 24 June 1844. SD

Edwards, C. C., of Jacksonville, and Charlotte Knowles, of Skaneateles, m. at Skaneateles, 31 Dec. 1851. SD

Edwards, J. Augustus, and Cornelia Rhoades, m. at Skaneateles, 18 May 1852. SD

Edwards, Jonathan, and Angeline Aldrich, both of Skaneateles, m. at Marcellus, 3 July 1849. SD

Edwards, Melzer, of Memphis, TN, and Frances Hecock, m. at Skaneateles, 19 Apr. 1852. SD

Edwards, Peter, of Skaneateles, m. Betsey Brosby, in Marcellus, (5 Jan.) 1831. OR

Edwards, Samuel, late of Skaneateles, now of Lamoille, IL, and Aurelia Maria Parmeter, of Pleasant Ridge, OH, m. 19 May 1842. SC

Edwards, Sobieski, and Harriet, dau. of George Coon, m. at Skaneateles, 4 June 1851. SC

Edwards, Thaddeus, of Skaneateles, and Maria, dau. of Nathan Clark, of Westhampton, m. 13 Nov. 1838. SC

Eeles, James W., and Caroline S., dau. of Silas Babcock, of Scott, m. at Homer, 6 Mar. 1845. SC

Egerton, John, of Pompey, and Angenetta Bump, of Fabius, m. at Fabius, 16 Mar. 1853.

Eggleston, Daniel, and Sarah Ann Robinson, m. at Clintonville, 11 May 1836. SC

Eggleston, Jerome, and Mary Ann VanValin, both of Skaneateles, m. at Auburn, 17 May 1840. SC

Eggleston, John, and Mary Ann, dau. of George Coon, of Skaneateles, m. 8 Jan. 1846. SC

Eggleston Theodore, of Skaneateles, and Sarah, dau. of Elder Gardner, m. at Venice, NY, 15 Sept. 1852. SD

Egleston, John, and Mrs. Catherine Elwood, m. at Lodi, 24 July 1828. SG&GA

Elderkin, Hiram Bromley, and Sarah Cornelia, dau. of Rogers Billings, all of Syracuse m. at Syracuse, 22 Sept. 1853. SD

Elliott, Charles, and Lucy Barber, both of Syracuse, m. at Syracuse, 4 Sept. 1837. SW

Elliott, E. J., of Syracuse, and Drusilla Dallman, of Salina, m. at Syracuse, 1 June 1846. SD

Elliott, George W., and Jane McKibbett, m. at Baldwinsville, 4 July 1853. SD
Elliott, J. Harris, and Jane Jones, both of VanBuren m. at Van Buren, 27 June 1853. SD
Ellis, John C. and Harriet Mann, m. at Onondaga, (19 Oct.) 1818.
Ellsworth, Thomas, and Jane Cole, m. at Sennett, 30 Apr. 1853.
Ellwood, J., and Mrs. A.E. Grimes, m. at Skaneateles, 3 Aug. 1850. SD
Elphick, George and Bridget Welch, m. at Skaneateles, 19 Mar. 1841. SC
Ely, Caleb, of Marcellus, and Elizabeth Russell, of Auburn, m. at Skaneateles, 7 Feb. 1838. SC
Ely, Caleb, and Elizabeth Ruggles, (see above) m. 9 Feb. 1838. STJ
Emery, Horatio Gates, of Milton, MA and Jane Tyler Brown, of Auburn m. at Auburn, 1 Nov. 1836. SC
Escott, Thomas, and Margaret Waldron, both of Skaneateles, m. at Auburn, 8 July 1845. SC
Estes, Gideon, and Emily Webster, m. in Pompey, (27 Jan.) 1830. OR
Evans, Asahel, and Zeziah (Keziah?) Weld, late of MA, m. in Pompey, 4 Nov. 1830. OR 17 Nov. [1830]
Everett, Milton S., and Mary E., only dau. of Ichabod Ross, all of Otisco, m 27 Feb. 1842. SC

F

Faber, Dr. R., of Logansport, IN, and Janet, dau. of Oliver R. Strong, m. at Onondaga, 14 Oct. 1851. SD
Fairchild, A. O., and Catharine Campbell, m. at Syracuse, 29 Oct. 1835. SC
Fairchild, William, and Catharine Badgley, both of DeWitt, m. at DeWitt, 25 Dec. 1853. SD
Fancher, Elisha S., and Sarah A. Kingsley, m. at Mexico, NY, 5 July 1838. SC
Farmer, Marcellus, of the Onondaga Standard, Jemimaette Tuttle, of Hempstead, Long Island, m. 1 Feb. 1842. SC
Farr, Joseph M., editor of the Ohio Experiment, and Malvina, dau. of the late Charles Jackson, of Onondaga Co., m. 17 May 1838. SC
Farrington, E., of Lysander, and Polly Haynes, of Camillus, m. -- Apr. 1825 SG
Farrington, Henry, of Chicago, and Almira Fellows, of Syracuse, m. at Chicago, 16 Oct. 1837. SW
Farwell, B. F. and Harriet, dau. of Alanson Edwards, m. at Syracuse, 31 May 1840. SC
Fay, Massilon W., and Caroline Welch, both of Skaneateles, m. at Mandana, 17 Oct. 1843. SC
Fenner, Turner, and Ruah Hickox, m. at Onondaga (16 Oct.) 1816. OR

Fenner, William Grove, and Hannah L. Stolp, m. at Marcellus, 19 Apr. 1847. SD

Field, Sereno, and Juliette, dau. of Thomas Reed, all of Skaneateles, m. at Skaneateles, 3 Oct. 1844. SC

Fields, Thomas J., of Syracuse, and Louisa A., dau. of the late Dr. Chapman, of Marcellus, m. at Syracuse, 23 May 1827. SA

Fiero, Stephen C., of Aurelius, and Nancy Stoner, of Owasco, m. at Owasco, 4 Nov. 1841. SC

Filkins, Barent, and Eliza Root, m. at Onondaga, (21 May) 1823. OR

Finch, Calvin, and Caroline S. Nash, of Syracuse, m. at Syracuse, 6 Jan. 1829. SG

Fink, William C. and Mary E., dau. of Henry Gifford, of Syracuse, m. at Syracuse, 6 Sept. 1853. SD

Fish, David, and Joanna Pickett, m. 15 Apr. 1838. STJ

Fish, Gilbert, of Syracuse, and Lydia Prentice, of Chester, MA, m. -- Jan. 1827. SA

Fisher, Thomas, of Skaneateles, and Harriet Hayler, m. at Marcellus, 17 Oct. 1853. SD

Fitch, George S., merchant, of Syracuse and Laura L., dau. of B. W. Cook, of Lenox, MA, m. in Lenox, 30 Aug. 1831. OR 7 Sept. [1831]

Fitch, Thomas B., and Ursula Ann Elliott, both of Syracuse, m. at Syracuse, 20 Oct. 1834. SC

Fitzgiles, Capt. Rueben, of Manchester, and Judah Sweeting, of Onondaga, m. at Onondaga, (28 Feb.) 1826. OR

Fleming, Thomas, and Nancy Ainsley, of Manlius, m. 26 Dec. 1826. SA

Flint, Cornelius, of Ira, and Elizabeth Cotton, of Camillus, m. at Camillus, 22 Jan. 1828. SA

Flower, George H. of Syracuse, and Sarah Fuller, of Lysander, m. at Little Utica, 20 May 1852. SD

Foltz, Peter, and Rosania F. Brenenstuhl, both of Manlius, m. at Manlius, 1 July 1828. SG&GA

Foot, Asahel, and Polly Britton, m. at Manlius, 22 Dec. 1828. SG&GA

Foot, Horace, of Manlius, and Angelica Whitmore, of Salina, m. at Manlius, 20 Oct. 1824. SG

Foot, Jared, and Eliza Clark, m. at Scipio, -- Jan. 1826. OR

Foot, Stephen, and ---- Teneur, of Owasco, m. at Owasco, 26 Dec. 1835. SC

Foote, Adam, and Mrs. Chapman, both of Elbridge, m. at Skaneateles, 25 Feb. 1851. SD

Foote, Perry, and Lodema, dau. of Eli Benedict, of Skaneateles, m. 21 Nov. 1844. SC

Foote, Stephen, and Mrs. Maria J. Shaw, m. at Spafford, 28 Oct. 1847. SC

Ford, Abraham, and Maria Wallace, m. at LeRoy, NY, (6 Oct.) 1819. OR

Ford, Charles, of Lawrenceville, PA, and Eliza M., dau. of the Hon. Daniel Kruger, of Syracuse, m. at Syracuse, 17 June 1830. OR, 25 June [1830]
Ford, Charles, of Marcellus, and Martha Gallup, of Skaneateles, m. at Skaneateles, 4 July 1853. SD
Ford, Martin M., Jr., of Syracuse, and Phebe Ann Parrish, of VanBuren, m. at VanBuren, 2 Apr. 1831. OR 6 Apr. [1831]
Forman, Daniel Ward, of Onondaga, and Elizabeth, dau. of Alexander Bliss, of Springfield, MA, m. at Springfield, (15 Feb.) 1820. OR
Fortescue, Thomas, of Rochester, and Margaret Monroe DeLancey, dau. of Bishop DeLancy, m. at Geneva, 6 May 1852. SD
Foster, Charles, and Jane M. Cuyler, both of Cortland, m. at Cortland, 13 Oct. 1853. SD
Foster, Joel, W., and Miss Rhoades, of Elbridge, m. at Elbridge, 17 Nov. 1852. SD
Foster, Solon, of Cicero, and Eliza Dorman, of Syracuse, m. at Syracuse, 19 Mar. 1840.
Foster, Theodore, of Skaneateles, and Henrietta D. B. Howell, of Marcellus, m. at Marcellus, 4 Oct. 1840. SC
Fowle, Edward J., Editor of the Yates County Republican, and Julia Smith, of Benton, m. 1 Apr. 1837. SA
Fowler, Azro, and Louisa A. Abbott, both of Skaneateles, m. at Skaneateles, 21 Dec. 1848. SD
Fowler, John S., and Maria, dau., of Alanson Benson, m. 13 Feb. 1845. SC
Fowler, John S., and Antha E. Abbott, both of Skaneateles, m. at the residence of Alanson Benson, of Skaneateles, 30 Oct. 1849. SD
Fowler, Samuel B., late of Skaneateles, and Mary Ann., dau. of John Powers, of Owasco, m. at Owasco, 3 Oct. 1837. SC
Fox, Almon, and Catharine Pierce, m. at Fabius. (4 May) 1826. OR
Fox, Henry, and Mary Hawke, both of Sempronius, m. at Auburn, -- -- 1852. SD
Francis, George, and Elizabeth C., dau. of Joseph Barber, both of Skaneateles, m. at Skaneateles, 11 May 1842. SC
Francis, Samuel, Sr., and Mrs. Sophia Cady, m. 5 Jan. 1833. STJ
Francis, Theron D., of Skaneateles. and Marion Terry, of Groton, NY, m. at Groton, ----. (1842-45?). SC
Frazer, K., of Syracuse, and Julia A. Richardson, of Otisco, m. at Otisco (2 Mar.) 1847. OD
French, A. J., and Mary Pomeroy, both of Syracuse, m. 15 May 1837. SW
French, Ashbel, Jr., and Jane R. Edwards, m. at Otisco, 16 Mar. 1852. SD
French, G. M., of Otisco, and Christiana Taylor, of Skaneateles, m. at Skaneateles, 28 Sept. 1848. SD
French, Dr. S. S., of Onondaga, and Ruth Adella, dau. of Silas Cox, of Otisco, m. 10 July 1842. SC
French, Sereno, of West Bloomfield, and Jane Elizabeth Whiting, of Richmond, NY, m. 14 May 1835. SC

Frisbie, Dr. D. G., and Mary C., dau. of Joseph Bulfinch, m. at Spafford, 14 Nov. 1845. SC

Frisbie, Myron J., and Joanna E. Delano, m. at Skaneateles, 10 Oct. 1837. SC

Frisby, David, and Juliet Woodbury, of Onondaga, m. 3 Feb. 1829. SG&GA

Frives, Emmil, and Mary Colanbrauer, late of Germany, m. at Syracuse, 9 Sept. 1851 ???

Frizzel, Horace, and Mary Ann Fuller, m. at Onondaga, 23 Feb. (Wed. last) 1820. OR

Frost, Ansel, and Minerva Noble, m. at Skaneateles, (18 Mar.) 1819. OR

Frost, C. A., late of Skaneateles, and Mary, dau. of Horace Griswold, of Delhi, NY, m. 17 Oct. 1843. SC

Fuller, Bonville, and Matilda Snook, dau. of Dr. John Snook, m. at Skaneateles, 9 Nov. 1847. SC

Fuller, Edward L., of MI, and Rosanna Truesdell, m. at Camillus, 27 Apr. 1834. SC

Fuller, Henry, and Mrs. Huldah VanEtten (?), dau. of Jacob VanEtten, m. at Skaneateles, 20 Jan. 1841. SC

Fuller, James, and Mary, dau. of John Snook, m. at Skaneateles, 31 Jan. 1846, SC

Fuller, Samuel, of Bath, England, son of J. C. Fuller, of Skaneateles, and Miss George, m. at Bath, Eng. 2 May 1846. SD

Fuller, Sumner, and Martha E., dau. of Richard Huxtable, m. at Skaneateles, 14 Sept. 1842. SD

Furgerson, Joseph S., and Mary Hopkins, m. at Camillus, 26 Oct. 1827. SA

G

Gage, James, and Betsey Perkins, both of Onondaga Valley, m. at Onondaga, (8 Mar) 1825. OR

Gale, Gillus V., and Fannie E. Darby, of Skaneateles, m. 12 Oct. 1843. SC

Gale, Thomas J., of Spafford, and Caroline, dau. of Norman Watson, of Skaneateles, m. 30 Dec. 1847. SC

Gallup, Benjamin, 2nd, of Camillus, and Freelove Phillips, of Homer, m. at Homer, 17 Oct. 1853. SD

Gallup, James, of Marcellus, and Charlotte P. Reed, late of England, m. at Skaneateles, 31 Mar. 1851. SD

Galusha, Ezra, of Homer, and Keturah VanHoosen, of Preble, m. at Preble, (16 Oct.) 1822. SD

Gardiner, John M., of Cleveland, OH, and Maria Hickok, of Skaneateles, m. at Skaneateles, 3 June 1846. SD

Gardner, Alonzo, and Sally N. Sanford, m. at Marcellus, 7 Mar. 1839. SC

Gardner, George J., and Phebe A. Teall, dau., of Oliver Teall, all of Syracuse, m. 10 Aug. 1843. SC

Gardner, H. C., and Marietta A. Mills, of Camillus, m. at Camillus, 14 Sept. 1853. SD

Gardner, Lyman, and Roxena Robinson, m. at Onondaga, (2 Sept.) 1822. OR

Gardner, Robert H., (m. 23 Dec. 1805, d. Medina, OH, 29 Sept. 1862) and Hannah Gardner (b. Greenwich, RI, 1 Apr. 1781; d. 9 Oct. 1825; bur. at Eagle Village (Manlius). Gardner Genealogy

Gardner, Sylvester (b. Hancock, MA, 11 Aug. 1770; d. Eagle Village, 30 July 1830); and Sarah Cogswell, (26 Feb. 1775 - 12 July 1853) m. 26 Apr. 1798. Came to Manlius 1810. Gardner Genealogy

Garlock, Josias, and Betsey Ann Shave, m. at Niles, 25 Dec. 1835. SC

Garrett, Albert, of Pompey, and Emily Daniels, of Rochester, m. at Rochester, 8 June 1852. SD

Gasquoine, Samuel, and Helen M. Dunbar, m. at Manlius (24 Dec.) 1846. OD

Gates, Lewis, of LeRoy, and Milicent Hall, m. 26 Sept. (Sun. eve last) 1819. OR 29 Sept. [1819]

Gay, Samuel, of Utica, and Nancy A. Newton, m in Skaneateles, (8 Dec.) 1830. OR

Gaylord, Leman R., of Otisco, and Catherine Mary, dau. of the Hon. John Spencer, of Cardiff, m. 19 Oct. 1847. SC

Gaylord, Levi B., and Clarissa Way, of Colchester, CT, m. at Otisco, 14 June 1841. SC

Geddes, George, of Onondaga, and Maria H., eldest dau. of Samuel Porter, m. in Skaneateles, 19 May 1830. OR, 26 May [1830]

Geddes, James of Fairmount, and Frances Terry, of Geddes, m. at Geddes, 24 Aug. 1853. SD

Geitner, Lewis, and Eunice Gage, m. at Onondaga, (12 Mar.) 1817, OR

German, George W., of MI, and Abigail B. Coates, of Otisco, m. -- June 1844. SC

Gifford, Dr. H., of Pompey, and Julia A. Ball, of Homer, m. at Homer, (29 Feb.) 1848. OD

Gifford, Stephen A., and Elizabeth L. Edwards, m. at Skaneateles, 19 Aug. 1851. SD

Gilbert, Daniel, of Salina, and Harriet Clark, of Pompey, m. at Pompey, (6 Sept.) 1817. OR

Gilbert, Nathaniel, of Sempronius, and Polly Enos, of Spafford, m. at Spafford, 2 June 1845. SC

Giles, Philander, and Jane Parks, both of Syracuse, m. at Syracuse, 19 Jan. 1853. SD

Giles, William P., of Skaneateles, and Lydia, dau. of James S. and Judith Allen, m. at Union Springs, 21 Dec. 1846. SD

Gilles, Archibald W., and Elsey Ann Cook, both of Camillus, m. at Camillus, (31 Dec.) 1825. OR

Gillet, Prosper J., of Clyde, and Delia A. Sellick, of Marcellus, m. at Auburn, 19 Feb. 1839. SC

Gilmore, Francis H., of Syracuse, and Frances R. Wilcox, of Baldwinsville, m. at Baldwinsville, 12 Mar. 1850. SD

Gilmore, William K. of Utica, and Caroline Kern, of Skaneateles, m. at Skaneateles, 18 Sept. 1848. SD

Glass, Daniel, and Ursula Coon, both of Skaneateles, m. at Auburn, 2 July 1846. SD

Glover, Daniel, and Harriet Miles, m. at Homer, 29 Mar. 1838. SC

Godard, William, of VA and Mary Morse, m. at Onondaga, (25 June) 1823. OR

Goddard, Peter, and Orpha Healy, both of Manlius, m. in Marcellus, 17 Mar. 1831. OR, 30 Mar. [1831]

Godfrey, John, of Auburn, and Eliza Mastin, of Syracuse, m. at Syracuse, 5 Jan. 1850. SD

Goff, Leonard, of Perryville, and Sarah M. Beeman, of Canasaraga, m. at Fayetteville, (20 June) 1847. OD

Gold, Thomas, of Whitesboro, and Martha Raymond, m. in Canton, St. Lawrence Co., NY, (16 Mar.) 1831. OR

Goodfellow, Samuel, and Barbara Row, both of Manlius, m. at Syracuse, 19 Jan. 1829. SG&GA

Goodrich, George, and Hannah Willey, m. at Syracuse, 15 May 1839. SC

Goodrich, George, and Lucy Hutchinson, both of Syracuse, m. at Syracuse, 6 July 1853. SD

Goodrich, Horace P., of Pittsfield, MA, and Mary Eliza, dau. of Myron L. Mills of Marcellus, m. at Marcellus, 5 Oct. 1843. SC

Goodsell, Charles, of Otsego Co., and Abigail Jennings of Manlius, m. at Manlius, (8 Oct.) 1830. OR

Goodwin, James D., of Otisco, and Mary Parker, of Spafford, m. at Spafford, 16 June 1840. SC

Goodwin, Leman B., of Otisco, and Minerva, dau. of Deac. Amaziah How, of Skaneateles, m. 21 Sept. 1843. SC

Gorham, Warren, of Elbridge, and Mary VanDewalker, also of Elbridge, m. at Auburn, 4 July 1850. SD

Gott, Daniel, and Mrs. Ann Sedgewick, m. at Pompey, (12 Sept.) 1819. OR

Gould, Amos, of Auburn, and Louisa H. Peck of Saratoga, m. at Saratoga Springs, 4 May 1841. SC

Gould, Edward O., and Mary, dau. of John N. Johnson, all of Syracuse, m. 11 Jan. 1844. SC

Gould, M. E., editor of the Cortland County Whig, and Mary Adaline, dau. of Lyman Scranton, m. at Utica, 1 June 1852. SD

Gould, Marshall, and Joyce Hunt, both of Onondaga, m. at Onondaga, (20 Feb.) 1825. OR

Gover, Samuel, of Skaneateles, and Betsey A. Wheatley, m. at Auburn, 10 Feb. 1853. SD

Graham, Andrew G., of Port Byron, and Maria E. Stevens, of Elbridge, m. at Elbridge, 1 Feb. 1844. SC

Grant, Lewis, and Betsey Allen, m. 5 Dec. 1835. STJ

Graves, Alexander, of Manlius, and Lydia Eastman of Pompey, m. in Pompey, (17 Nov.) 1830. OR
Graves, Lewis, of CT, and Adelphia D. Baker, of Marcellus, m. at Marcellus, 20 Sept. 1848. SD
Graves, Sheldon, and Mary, dau. of Clark Camp, of Jordan, m. at Jordan, (12 Jan.) 1847. OD
Gray, Henry A., of Nunda, NY, and Mary A. Purchase, of Spafford, m. at Spafford, 7 May 1851. SD
Green, Andrew, and Maria Taylor, m. at Skaneateles, 27 Feb. 1840. SC
Green, Dr. Caleb, of Homer, and Anna R., dau. of Levi Parsons, of Northampton, MA, m. -- Sept. 1845. SC
Green, Norman, of Onondaga, and Julia Sparks, of Otisco, m. at Otisco, 21 Oct. 1824. OR
Green, Russell, of Owasco, and Rebecca P. Austin, of Moravia, m. at Moravia, 14 Apr. 1852. SD
Green, Thomas, of Manlius, and Calista Colton (or Cotton), m. at Marcellus, (5 Jan.) 1820. OR
Green, Turpin, and Patty Hall, m. at Pompey, (7 Jan.) 1819. OR
Greenfield, DeWitt C., and Harriet Foster, both of VanBuren, m. -- Mar. 1841. SC
Greenman, S. H., of Skaneateles, and Sarah Mason, of Jordan. m. at Jordan, 14 Jan. 1850. SD
Gregg, ----, and Juliet Peck, m. 7 May 1835. SC
Gregory, David G., and Sarah Rhodes, m. at Skaneateles, (8 Dec.) 1830. OR
Gregory, Joshua, of Skaneateles, and Elizabeth Rishmore, of Sennett, m. 17 June 1848. SD
Grey, Clark, and Almira Walch, both of Marietta, m. at Tully, 28 May 1840. SC
Gridley, Rueben, of Onondaga Hollow, and Julia Morgan of Truxton, m. at Pompey, 19 May 1831. OR, 25 May [1831]
Griffin, Charles G., and Mary Fuller, both of Onondaga, m. at Camillus, 16 Jan. 1845. SC
Griffin, Harvey C., of Otisco, and Rebecca Jane Abbott, of Marcellus, m. at Marcellus, (16 Sept.) 1846. OD, also SD
Griffin, Henry, and Samantha Dodge, m. at Onondaga, (21 Feb.) 1816. OR
Griffin, Lyman, of Otisco, and Ruth, dau. of Daniel Nickerson, late of Skaneateles, m. -- June 1837. SC
Griffin, Samuel, and Roxena Tripp, m. at Cicero, -- May 1826. OR
Griswold, Franklin L., and Laura H., dau. of Rev. Dr. Lansing, m. at Auburn, 15 May 1838. SC
Griswold, Gaylord, of Buffalo, and Harriet Root, m. at Jordan, 12 Apr. 1852. SD
Griswold, Lt. Samuel B., of the 2nd U.S.A. Inf., and Catherine W., dau. of Arthur Breese, m. at Utica (26 Jan.) 1820. OR
Groome, Volney B., of Skaneateles, and Mahala DeWaters, of Elbridge, m. at Jordan, 2 Feb. 1851. SD

Grover, Harmon, of Owasco, and Sarah Owen, of Sennett, m. 4 Mar. 1837. SC

Guilford, Alvin, and Louisa, dau. of Martin Ford of Camillus, m. 10 Apr. 1827. SA

Gunn, Lucius, and Amy Smith, m. in Marcellus, (16 Feb.) 1831. OR

Guppy, William, and Ann Carrington, m. at Skaneateles, 6 Feb. 1844. SC

Gurnee, Col. Abraham S., of Auburn, and Sarah Jane, dau. of Henry Severn, of Sempronius, m. 20 Oct. 1842 (or 40?). SD

Gurney, John, of St. Albans, OH, and Ruth Pierson, of Auburn, m. at Skaneateles, 25 May 1840. SC

Gurnsey, Dr. Jonathan, and Miss Furman, of Madison, m. 1 Jan. 1820. OR, 5 Jan. [1820]

H

Hadger, Joseph, and Prudence Spaulding, m. at Geddes, -- July 1827. SA

Haeker, George, and Hannah Reynor, m. 28 Sept. 1835. STJ

Hager, Rev. Elijah W., of Washington, DC, and Mary Jane Huxtable, of Skaneateles, m. 18 Feb. 1843. SC

Haight, Nathaniel, and Maria Burns, both of Skaneateles, m. at Skaneateles, 26 June 1851. SD

Haight, Samuel W., of San Francisco, and Juliet Eulen Croswell, dau. of Edwin Croswell, m. at New York City, 14 Jan. 1852. SD

Haight, Seth, proprietor of the Cortland Democrat, and Calista, dau. of Danforth Merrick, of Cortland, m. 20 Dec. 1843. SC

Hale, Ambrose, and Elizabeth Larkin, both of Liverpool, m. 28 Feb. 1824. OG

Hales, Seth W., of New York, and Fannie Jewett Richards, second dau. of J. M. Richards, of Syracuse, m. 15 Oct. 1853. SD

Hall, Charles F., of Salem, MA, and Almira Bird, of Skaneateles, m. at Skaneateles, 31 Jan. 1844. SC

Hall, David, and Lydia, dau. of Eli Benedict, of Skaneateles, m. 21 Nov. 1844. ???

Hall, David, 2nd, and Mary L. Allis, both of Skaneateles, m. at Skaneateles, 29 Sept. 1841. SC

Hall, George S., and Jeanette Leonard, m. at Auburn, (23 Feb.) 1831. OR

Hall, Hopestill, and Eliza Sparks, both of Onondaga, m. at Pompey, (20 Mar.) 1823. OR

Hall, Israel, of Camillus, and Olive Bigelow, dau. of Judge Otis Bigelow, of Baldwinsville, m. 28 May 1848. SC

Hall, James M., and Harriet M. Holden, both of Fulton, m. at Fulton, (28 June) 1847. OD

Hall, John, and Jane Wright, m. at Onondaga, 4 May 1843. SD

Hall, John A., of Marcellus, and Betsey Rogers, of Auburn, m. at
    Auburn, (31 May) 1820. OR
Hall, Jonathan, and Polly Andrews, m. at Pompey, (7 Jan.) 1819. OR
Hall, Joseph of Otisco, and Polly Crosby, m. at Marcellus (5 Jan.)
    1831. OR
Hall, L. W., and Mary Elizabeth, dau. of William Clark, of Syracuse,
    m. at Syracuse, 27 Feb. 1851. SD
Hall, Lemuel, of Marietta, and Jane Hewett, of Vesper, m. 26 July
    1851. SC
Hall, Samuel W., formerly of Cicero, and Ariyet, dau. of Col. Bienrjice,
    of Smithfield, m. at Syracuse, 16 Nov. 1824. SG
Hall, Seth F., of Skaneateles, and Lucy E. Alvord, of Jordan, m. at
    Jordan, 16 Sept. 1841. SC
Hall, T. Jefferson, and Francesca, dau. of P. P. Cleveland, late of
    Skaneateles, m. at Syracuse, 2 June 1850. SD
Halladay, John, and Polly Cortright, m. at Auburn, 6 Sept. 1836. SC
Halstead, William, and Clarissa Hall, both of Springport, m. 14 Dec.
    1826. AFP
Hamilton, William T., of Syracuse, and Fannie M., dau. of Gardner
    Lawrence, late of Syracuse, m. at Syracuse, 20 June 1853. SD
Hamlin, Dor, of Auburn, and Amelia, J., dau. of M. A. Kinney, m. at
    Skaneateles, 19 Oct. 1853. SD
Hamlin, Monroe, of Owasco, and Mahala Cox, of Aurelius, m. at
    Aurelius, 25 Jan. 1843. SC
Hamlin, Col. S. H., of Owasco, brother of Mrs. J. H. Smith of Skan-
    eateles, and Charity, dau. of Moses Cuykendall, m. at Skane-
    ateles, 18 Dec. 18 Dec. 1850, by Rev. Nelson Cuykendall. SD
Hamilton, Alexander, and Caroline, dau. of E. E. Austin, of Skaneate-
    les, m. at Skaneateles, 24 Oct. 1848. SD
Hammond, Samuel H., of Salina, and Emeline Humphrey, of Nine Mile
    Creek, m. at Nine Mile Creek, 3 Sept. 1828.. SG&GA
Hanchett, Dr. John C., of Syracuse, and Juliet Hanks, of Troy, m. at
    Troy, 31 Aug. 1831. OR, 7 Sept. [1831]
Hand, Joseph, and Charity Fletcher, m. at Auburn, 18 Sept. 1846. OD
Hanford, Edward, of CT, and Frances Shepherd, of Auburn, m. at
    Auburn, 11 Mar. 1827. AFP
Hanna, Robert, of Lewiston, PA, and Mary Phillips, of Syracuse, m. 4
    May 1837. SW
Hannum, James, of Skaneateles, and Frances, dau. of E. Rowley, of
    Marcellus, m. at Marcellus, 6 Oct. 1852. SD
Harble, A., U.S.A. and Margaret Hunter, niece of Gen. R. B. Mason,
    U.S.A., m. at St. Louis, MO, 11 Mar. 1851. SD
Hardy, James, and Miss C. Wilsey, m. at Springfield, Otsego Co., 1
    Nov. 1826. SA
Harmance, Dr. L., of Auburn, and Sarah Ferris, of Ithaca, m. at
    Ithaca, 18 Apr. 1839. SC
Harris, Burlingame, and Sarah Spalding, m. at Borodino, 1 Jan., 1838.
    SC

Harris, George W., and Mrs. Lucinda Morgan, widow of the late Capt. William Morgan, m. at Batavia, (8 Dec.) 1830. OR

Harrison, Frederick, of Albany, and Sarah Laton, of Auburn, m. at Auburn, 16 Apr. 1839. SC

Harrod, Thomas, of Scott, and Margaret, dau. of John Vosburgh, of Marcellus, m. at Marcellus, 7 June 1838. SC

Harwood, Hiram, and Jane E., dau. of Peregrine White, of Skaneateles, m. at Skaneateles, 30 June 1852. SD

Harwood, M., and L. Chatfield, both of Skaneateles, m. at Skaneateles, 4 Sept. 1851. SD

Haskin, Lansing G., and Mary Ann Rowe, both of Salina, m. at Salina, (1 Jan.) 1826. OR

Haskins, Enoch, and Hannah B. Hall, both of Skaneateles, m. 13 Dec. 1843. SC

Haslett, Charles, of Brutus, and Sarah S. Sheldon, of Cato, m. at Skaneateles, 21 Dec. 1847. SC

Hatch, Henry, and Adeline Colvin, m. at Syracuse, 13 June 1849. SD

Hatch, Capt. John P., of the U.S.A., and Adeline G., dau. of Charles J. Buckle, m. at Oswego, 14 June 1851. SD

Hatch, Revilo C., of Fayetteville, and Mary, dau. of Philip Flint, of Watertown, m. at Syracuse, (5 Aug.) 1846. OD

Hausinfrates, Mr. of Syracuse, and Harriet Wheatley, m. at New York City, 21 Nov. 1829. OR 9 Dec. [1829]

Haven, Thomas and Clarissa Ann Jackson, m. at Auburn, 30 Sept. 1838. SC

Hawley, A. Hamilton, and Mary E., widow of the late Addison Howe, of Skaneateles, m. at Dimant Springs, CA, 13 June 1853. SD

Hawley, Cyrus W., and Helen Gold, of Pompey, m. at Manlius, -- June 1826. OR

Hawley, Nelson, and Cornelia, dau. of Samuel Francis, m. at Skaneateles, 22 Jan. 1834. SC and STJ

Hawley, Samuel T., of New England, and Grace Anderson, of Nine Mile Creek, Camillus, m. 1 Aug. 1824. SG

Hay, William, and Margaret Ladd, both of Camillus, m. at Camillus, 22 Nov. 1827. SA

Haynes, Sylvester, and Almira Dunham, both of Lysander, m. at Camillus, 24 Feb. 1853. SD

Hazard, James, of Onondaga, and Emeline S. Webster, of LaFayette, m. at LaFayette, (8 Sept.) 1846. OD

Healey, Edwin, M. D., late of Marcellus, and Maria, dau. of Capt. William Thomas, m. at Skaneateles, 13 Mar. 1838. SC

Hecox, Armon, and Olive Putnam, m. 5 Mar. 1837. STJ

Hecox, Col. Warren, and Polly Weston, both of Skaneateles, m. 22 Dec. 1844. SC

Hecox, Wesley, and Miss Story, both of Syracuse, m. 15 May 1837. SW

Hemseed (Hemsted?) James, and Mrs. Louisa Owen, of Marietta, m. at Syracuse, 22 June 1845. SC

Hemstead, E. A., and Abby, dau. of Mather B. Church, of Baldwinsville, m. at Baldwinsville, 17 Dec. 1853. SD
Henn, J. H., of Syracuse, and P. B. Hough, m. at Manlius, 20 July 1852. SD
Henry, John T., of New York, and Elvenah M., dau. of Jedidiah Barber, m. at Homer, 19 July 1838. SC
Hermanse, Thomas, of Syracuse, and Annie, dau. of John G. Fobbes (or Forbes), m. at Syracuse, 18 Oct. 1853. SD
Herrick, O. B., of Camillus, and Anna Scoville, of Pompey, m. at Pompey, -- Jan. 1829. SG&GA
Herrick, Origan W., of Baldwinsville, and Rosetta R., dau. of R. U. Smith, m. at Belleville, Canada West, 19 Apr. 1853. SD
Herring, James, and Charlotte, dau. of Curtis Moses, all of Marcellus, m. at Marcellus, 17 June 1846. SD
Herrington, A. H., and Phebe Peck, both of Jordan, m. at Jordan, 19 Sept. 1831. SC
Herrington, Henry H., M. D., and Nancy M. Remington, m. at Manlius, 23 Sept. 1839. SC
Hewes, Shubel E., and Henrietta B. White, a teacher, of Syracuse, m. at Syracuse, 27 Dec. 1853. SD
Hibbard, F., of Waterloo, and Phebe Hamilton of Onondaga, m. at Onondaga, (20 Jan) 1847. OD
Hibbard, John E., of Onondaga, and Matilda, dau. of E. Robbins, of Syracuse, m. at Syracuse, 23 Sept. 1846. OD
Hicks, Walter, and Harriet A. Davis, m. at Marietta, 30 Dec. 1841. SC
Higby, Levi J., and Sally Clemons, m. at Pompey, (27 Jan.) 1830. OR
Higgins, Hiram, of Borodino, and Mary Ann, dau. of Thomas Bennett, of Syracuse, m. at Syracuse, 2 Oct. 1838. SC
Higgins, John, of Salina, and Mary J. Kinney, of Syracuse, m. at Syracuse, (23 Jan.) 1847. OD
Higgs, Benjamin, and Elizabeth, dau. of Richard Davis, all of Skaneateles, m. 26 June 1845. SC
Higley, Jacob S. and Delina M. Spencer, m. at Onondaga Valley, (9 Nov.) 1822. OR
Hill, Timothy, and Marianne Radford, m. 9 Sept. 1837. STJ
Hill, Timothy, of Otisco, and Jane Reeves, of Skaneateles, m. at Sennett, -- July 1846. SD
Hiller, Isaac, of Jamestown, NY, and Cynthia Ann Osborn, of Borodino, m. 7 Sept. 1841. SC
Hilliard, David, and Sally Ann (Sarah A.) Cuddeback, m., at Skaneateles, 26 or 27 Feb. 1838. SC also STJ
Hilliard, John, and Josephine Burdick, m. at Skaneateles, 4 Nov. 1848. SD
Hilliard, Van Rensselaer, and Ruth Kellog, both of Skaneateles, m. at Skaneateles, 19 Apr. 1835. SC
Hilliard, William D., and Susan DeWitt, m. at Niles, 15 Nov. 1835. SC
Hills, Elezear, merchant, of Auburn, and Sarah W., dau. of Josiah Bissell, of Pittsfield, MA, m. at Pittsfield, 16 Sept. 1819. OR, 6 Oct. [1819]

Hillyer, Myron, and Philinda (Philanda) Griffin, both of Amber, m. at Amber, 27 Apr. 1851. SD

Hines, Henry, of Hartsville, and Eliza A. Nettleton, of Syracuse, m. at Syracuse, (28 Jan.) 1847. OD

Hiscock, Henry, late of Tully, and Frances M. Willard, m. at North Plains, MI 8 Dec. 1853. SD

Hitchcock, Josiah W., of Skaneateles, and Sylvia Parmeter, m. at Cortland, 4 July 1838. SC

Hitchcock, Julius, of Mexico, NY and Susan Drake, of Onondaga Hollow, m. at Syracuse, 24 May 1827. SA

Hitchins, Warren, and Eunice Ann Knapp, m. 10 Mar. 1839. STJ

Hoag, Henry, and Catharine Balch, both of Skaneateles, m. at Syracuse, 22 Dec. 1853. SD

Hoagland, Josiah Y., of Skaneateles, and Ann B. Canfield, of Auburn, m. at Auburn, 4 Apr. 1850. SD

Hoar, Leonard, and Abbey Whitney, m. at Pompey, 11 Dec. 1831. SC

Hobart, Charles W., and Philena Singerland, of Fabius, m. at Cortland, 23 May 1853. SD

Hobby, J. C. A., late of Skaneateles, and Sophia Ann, dau. of Philander Mead, of Milan, NY, m. 20 Aug. 1845. SC

Hobert, Jacob H., of Cicero, and Martha Holliday, of Canastota, m. in Lenox, 4 Apr. 1830. OR 28 Apr. [1830]

Hoffman, John A., of Skaneateles, and Jane A. Homes, of Auburn, m. at Auburn, 30 Mar. 1843. SC

Holbrook, Dwight, of OH, and Lydia Ann, dau. of B. F. VanTyne, of Elbridge, m. at Cleveland, OH, 22 June 1842. SC

Holbrook, George, and Sally Cadwell, m. at Manlius, (12 Mar.) 1817. OR

Holbrook, Jerome B., and Frances L. Conner, both of Syracuse, m. at Syracuse, 3 Nov. 1853. SD

Holcomb, Elam, of Syracuse, and Mary Jacoby, m. at Zion Church in Butternuts, 6 May 1827. SA

Hollister, Lucius M., of Cato, and Sarah M., dau. of Josiah Smith, of Lysander, m. at Lysander, 18 June 1840. SC

Honeywell, John, and Margaret Whittaum, m. at Skaneateles, 8 July 1838. SC (NB: Her name is given as Mary Whittum in STJ.)

Hooker, Dr., of Salina, and Mary Beardslee, of Auburn, m. at Auburn, 6 Feb. 1827. SA

Hopkins, Aaron, and Ann Marie Shelton, both of Camillus, m. at Syracuse, 5 June 1830. OR 9 June [1830]

Hopkins, Batton, M. and Margaret McDougall, both of Syracuse, m. at Syracuse, 3 May 1850. SD

Hopkins, L. S., of Marathon, and Sally Gumaer, of Skaneateles, m. at Skaneateles, 14 May 1846. SD

Hopkins, Willett, and Maria Lynch, both of Cicero, m. 18 Oct. 1828. SG&GA

Hooper, George, and Ann Robbins, m. at Onondaga, 20 Apr. 1830. OR 28 Apr.[1830]

Horton, Henry B, of Mansfield, OH, and Addie L., dau. of Hon. N. S. Holobird, m. at Winsted, CT, 5 May 1851. SD

Hoskins (or Haskins), Alson G., of Marcellus, and Rosaline H. Chase, of Howlett Hill, m. at Howlett Hill, 2 Jan. 1844. SC

Hoskins (or Haskins), George, of Skaneateles, and Caroline Bentliff, of Utica, m. at Utica, 12 Sept. 1851. SD

Hoskins, James W. of New York, and Henrietta Cuddeback, of Skaneateles, m. at Skaneateles, 4 Sept. 1851. SD

Hosmer, C. Mark, of the Onondaga Gazette, Baldwinsville, and H. Janette Parsons, of VanBuren, m. at VanBuren, 4 Feb. 1851. SD

Hosmer, James W., and Eliza Betts, of Jordan, m. 22 May 1842. SC

Hotchkiss, Dr. Benjamin, and Delia Baldwin, both of Otisco, m. at Otisco, 25 Sept. 1842. SC

Hotchkiss, David, of Syracuse, and Julia M. Howard, of Skaneateles, m. at Skaneateles, 25 Mar. 1852. SD

Hotchkiss, Henry, and Cynthia Steward, both of Amber, m. at Amber, 5 Jan. 1852. SD

Hotchkiss, Miles, and Susan Sheldon, both of Cicero, m. 19 July 1823. OG

Hough, Amos B., and Sarah A. Wallace, both of Syracuse, m. at Syracuse, (4 Mar.) 1847. OD

Hough, Ezra H., and Lucy Brackett, m. at Syracuse, 19 Dec. 1837. SW

Houghtaling, Asa, and Phebe Houghtaling, m. at Pompey, (7 Jan.) 1819. OR

Houghtaling, Col. James, and Amy Raymond, m. at Lafayette, 8 Feb. 1839. SC

House, Anson, and Lucinda, dau. of Capt. Ezra Blossom, m. at Brighton, Ontario Co., (26 Jan.) 1820. OR

Hovey, Alexander R., and Almira Brown, both of Syracuse, m. at Syracuse, 13 Sept. 1831. OR, 21 Sept. [1931]

How, Addison, of Skaneateles, and Ruama, dau. of Marcus Goodwin, of Otisco, m. at Otisco, 1 Jan. 1844. SC

How, William, and Henrietta G., dau. of Ebenezer Cobb, both of Auburn, m. at Auburn, 8 Oct. 1846. SD

Howard, Rev. G. A., of MA, and Sarah T. Chidney (or Chidsey), of Florence, NY, m. at Skaneateles, 30 Apr. 1846. SD and also OD

Howard, Ransom, and Melinda McComley (or McComby), m. at Marcellus, (19 Jan.) 1831. OR

Howard, Sylvester, and Clarissa Clark, m. at Skaneateles, 3 May 1838. SC

Howe, Addison, and Mary E., dau. of Manly Hitchcock, all of Skaneateles, m. at Skaneateles, 24 Nov. 1852. SD. See also How, Addison.

Howe, P. Dean, and D. C. Lyman, m. at Marcellus, 20 Oct. 1846. SC

Howey, (Hovey?) E., of Skaneateles, and Frances Crippen, of Auburn, m. at Throopsville, 2 June 1850. SD

Howland, William, of Scipio, and Hannah Maria, dau. of J. Letchworth, of Auburn, m. at Auburn 26 Apr. 1853. SD

Howlett, Horatio G., and Amanda M., dau. of Joel Canfield, m. at Syracuse, 31 Aug. 1830. OR 1 Sept. [1830]

Hoxie, Rowland, and Lucy Griffen, m. at Marcellus, 13 Oct. 1841. SC

Hoyt, Day B., and Lydia E. Stolp, m. at Onondaga, 8 Apr. 1875. SD

Hoyt, Ezekiel G., and Mary, dau. of Howard Delano, m. at Mottville, 14 Oct. 1851. SD

Hoyt, Rufus, of Sennett, and Hannah Pattee, m. at Owasco, 7 Jan. 1845. SC

Hoyt, Thomas, and Minerva Baker, m. at Lafayette, 26 May 1830. OR

Hubbard, Alexander, of Syracuse, and Jane Wood, of Navarino, m. at Navarino, 29 Mar. 1850. SD

Hubbard, Enos, and Nancy Brown. m. at Onondaga, (12 Sept.) 1822. OR

Hubbard, Oran, and Hannah Furman, m. -- Feb. 1818. OR

Hubbard, Oren, and Hannah Furman, m. at Lysander, -- Feb. 1818. OR

Hubbell, Charles, of Fulton, and Maria G. Vedder, of Lysander, m. at Skaneateles, 13 Aug. 1846. SD

Hudson, Philander W., and Eliza VanSlyke, both of Syracuse, m. at Syracuse, 10 Apr. 1831. OR 13 Apr. [1831]

Hughes, Arthur, and Beulah Gould, both of Onondaga, m. at Syracuse, 23 Sept. 1830. OR 6 Oct. [1830]

Humphrey, Theron, late of Skaneateles, and Charlotte Casell, of Auburn, m. at Seneca Falls, 28 June 1834. SC

Hungerford, Stephen R., and Mary J. Bush, both of Lafayette, m. at Syracuse, (16 Sept.) 1847. OD

Hunsiker, Elias, of Skaneateles, and Mary E. Halt, of Seneca Falls, m. at Skaneateles, -- Feb. 1853. SD

Hunsiker, Henry, and Harriet Deckerman, m. -- Jan. 1835. STJ

Hunt, C. H., and Eliza Lathrop, m. at Syracuse, 5 July 1838. SC

Hunt, David, and Ginnet Terry, m. in Onondaga, 24 Feb. 1831. OR, 9 May. [1831]

Hunt, Jasper, and Ann M. Brill, m. at Marcellus, 2 Jan. 1844. SC

Hunt, Wallace, and Martha Bennett, of Auburn, m. at Auburn, 17 May 1853. SD

Hunt, Isaac, and Sarah Hare, both of Manlius, m. at Salina, 1 Jan. 1824. OG

Hunter, Nathaniel, of Cato, and Roxey Lewis, of Skaneateles, m. at Skaneateles 2 (or 3) Feb. 1836. SC

Huntington, William E., of Baldwinsville, and Elizabeth Safford, of VanBuren, m. at VanBuren, 10 Nov. 1853, SD

Huntely, Lentulus, and Henrietta Hicks (or Wicks), m. at Onondaga, (12 Sept.) 1822. OR

Hurbard (Hubbard?), J. M., of Springfield, MA, and Miss S. A. Blakeley, of the Blakeley Vocalists, of Syracuse, m. at East Berkshire, VT, 17 Oct. 1853. SD

Hurd, John H., and Mary A. Fries, both of Auburn, m. at Auburn, 16 Nov. 1853. SD

Hutchins, Phineas, Jr., and Hannah E., dau. of John R. Lewis, of Spafford, m. 3 Feb. 1846. SC

Hutchinson, James, and Frances Ann Downey, both of Marcellus, m. at Marcellus, 29 Dec. 1841. SC

Hutchinson, John, and Matilda A. Smith, both of Salina, m. at Salina 2 Dec. 1841. SC

Hyde, Hiram, and Mary E., dau. of Joshua Forman, m. at Syracuse, 25 Jan. 1824. OG

Hyde, Porter W., and Alicia Lanes (or Leynes) m. at Salina, 9 Sept. 1827. SA

Hyde, Simeon (1742-1789) and Dorothy St. John (b. Wilton, CT, 14 Nov. 1742, d. at Skaneateles, 8 Feb. 1839; mother of Mrs. D. Kellog); m. 1864 [sic] (1764?). (Whitney Genealogy)

I

Ingison, Hiram, of Clay, and Emily A. Tuttle of Otisco, m. 14 Feb. 1848. SC

Inglish [English], Charles, and Electa Johnson, m. 1 Sept. 1842. SC

Irwin, Charles, and Caroline, dau. of Pontius Hooper, m. at Waterloo, NY (22 Sept.) 1819. OR

Ivison, John C., and Harriet M. Withey, m. at Auburn, 12 Oct. 1842. SC

J

Jackson, Albin, and Amanda Bradley, m. at Onondaga, (3 Apr.) 1823. OR

Jackson, Falk, and Elizabeth Queen, m. at Syracuse, 17 Oct. 1841. SC

Jacobs, Calvin, of Pompey, and Mary A. West, of Onondaga, m. (24 Nov.) 1824. OR

James, Thomas I., of the Madison County Journal, and Adeline Marble, of Syracuse, m. at Syracuse, 14 Oct. 1830. OR, 20 Oct. [1830]

Janes, Ebenezer, Jr., and Phebe Wells, of Onondaga, m. at Geddes, (6 Feb.) 1825. OR

Jaqueth, Sampson F., and Julia, dau. of W. A. Crawford, m. at Liverpool, (16 Dec.) 1846. OD

Jaquin, Peter, and Susan Thorout, both of Salina, m. at Salina, (2 Jan.) 1847. OD

Jaris, Henry A., and Lydia A. Boynton, both of McLean, m. at Homer, 29 Jan. 1853. SD

Jay, William H., of Marcellus, and Jane Rich, of Skaneateles, m. at Skaneateles, 28 Feb. 1835. SC and STJ

Jefferds, George H., and Sally Chamberlain, both of Fulton, m, at Fulton, (31 Jan.) 1847. OD

Jeffers, Henry P., of Skaneateles, and Melvina Potter, of Camillus, m. at Camillus, 22 Dec. 1839. SC

Jerome, Aaron, of Jamesville, and Nancy Wells, m. at Camillus, (9 Sept.) 1819. OR

Jerome, Addison G., of New York, and Julia, dau. of Phares Gould, of Skaneateles, m. at Skaneateles, 2 July 1840. SC

Jerome, Charles L. of Rochester, and Susan M., dau. of William Brown of Sennett (?), m. at Auburn, 13 May 1856 (or 1851). SD

Jewett, William H., of Skaneateles, and Eliza, dau. of John Riddle, m. at Wilmington, DE, 26 May 1842. SD

Jewhurst, Edward B., and Jane Lynd, both of Auburn, m. at Auburn, 11 Aug. 1852. SD

Jilson, Whipple, of Elbridge, and Caroline Bayles, of Weedsport, m. at Weedsport, (9 Sept) 1846. OD

Johnson, Gardner, of Verona, and Fanny Cook, of Salina, m. at Salina, (1 Dec.) 1830. OR

Johnson, John H., and Lucia Hutchinson, m. at Onondaga, (5 Jan.) 1820. OR

Johnson, John W., and J. G. Colson, both of Elbridge, m. at Elbridge, 10 Mar. 1847. SD

Johnson, Norman B., of Pompey, and Mrs. Nancy L. Long, of Syracuse, m. at Syracuse, (3 Feb.) 1847. OD

Johnson, O. E., and Celia, dau. of James Chappell, m. at Auburn, 28 Aug. 1849. SD

Johnson, Rodney, and Betsey Cramer, m. at Pompey, (6 Oct.) 1819. OR

Johnson, William A., of Syracuse, and Hannah Lovejoy, of Chatham, NY, m. at Chatham, -- Oct, 1827. SA

Johnston, Charles H., of Otisco, and Rebecca Ann, dau. of George Christler, of Marcellus, m. 1 Jan. 1845. SC

Johnston, Rev. James, and Mary Cox, m. at Auburn, 10 Oct. 1839. SC

Jones, Byron W., and Frances Kasson, both of Baldwinsville, m. at Baldwinsville, 13 Dec. 1852. SD

Jones, Cornelius R., of Trenton, NY (?) and Phebe Barbour, m. in Lodi, 28 Nov. 1831. OR 30 Nov. [1831]

Jones, Dr. Daniel T., of Baldwinsville, and Eliza, dau. of James R. Lawrence, of Syracuse, m. 30 June 1841. SC

Jones., E., and Polly Mary Taylor of Skaneateles, m. at Skaneateles, 16 Nov. 1843. SC

Jones, Franklin O., and Ellen Henderson, both of Skaneateles, m. at Auburn, 5 Oct. 1836. SC

Jones, Henry, and Polly Merrian, m. in Cicero, (17 Feb.) 1830. OR

Jones, Henry, and Henrietta Davey, m. 3 July 1839. STJ

Jones, Lewis, and Mary Hawley, both of Aurelius, m. at Skaneateles, 13 Jan. 1846. SC

Jones, Peter, Jr., of Marcellus, and Harriet Sandiforth, m. in Utica, (6 Oct.) 1830. OR
Jones, Richard T., and Elizabeth A. Kenyon, m. at Fulton, (24 Aug.) 1846. OD
Jones, William, and Rebecca Harris, m. at Onondaga, (12 Mar.) 1817. OR
Joslin, Dr. Hezekiah, of Cicero, and Helen Leslie, late of Auburn, m. at Cicero, 15 Feb. 1825. SG
Josselyn, Seth, and Hannah Aumock, m. at Otisco, (15 Feb.) 1815. OR
Judd, Alvin, and Mrs. Lucinda Mitchell, of Salina, m. in Salina 28 Nov. 1830. OR, 1 Dec. [1830]
Judd, S. Corning, of the Syracuse Star, and Lavina L. James, dau. of the late William James, of Washington, DC, m. at Washington, DC, 30 June (or 5 July) 1852. SD
Judson, Rev. Adoniram, D. D., and Emily A. Chubbuck, m. at Hamilton, NY, -- May 1846. SC
Julia, William H., and Mary Ann Ruff, both of Skaneateles, m. at Syracuse, 30 July 1849. SD

Kain, Morris, and Catharine Traffagan, both of Salina, m. at Salina, 22 Feb. 1825. SG
Kaisir, Pius, and Ann Pinchler, both late of Germany, m. at Syracuse, 9 Sept. 1851. SD
Kate, Charles, and Maria Caple, m. at Syracuse, 7 Apr. 1848. SC
Kearn, Henry, and Mary Dummitt, late of Skaneateles, m. at Auburn, 6 Mar. 1848. SC
Keeler, J. E. of Sennett, and Laura E., eldest dau. of Harmon Cole, m. at Skaneateles, 9 Nov. 1853. SD
Keeler, James, of Onondaga, and Nancy Dings, of DeWitt, m. at DeWitt, (5 Jan.) 1847. OD
Keeler, Myron T., of Syracuse, and Emeline, dau. of Jabin Armstrong, of Helle Isle, m. 27 Dec. 1853. SD
Keeney, Jonathan O., of Skaneateles, and Caroline N., dau. of William R. Peacock, of the same place, m. at Skaneateles, 23 Oct. 1849 SD
Keep, John A., of Homer, and Cornelia A. Reynolds, of Westfield, NY, m. at Westfield, 8 May 1839. SC
Keep, William, of Lockport, and Frances S., dau. of Harvey Rhoades, of Syracuse, m. 4 Aug. 1841. SD
Kelby, James, of Niles, and Dinah Ellsbury, of Skaneateles, m. at Skaneateles, 30 Sept. 1852. SD
Kellogg, Augustine, and Chloe Tefft, m. at Baldwinsville, 8 May 1840. SC
Kellog, Augustine, of Baldwinsville, and Mrs. Emeline Hatch, m. at Onondaga, 17 Nov. 1845. SC

Kellogg, Augustus, of Skaneateles, and Cornelia C., dau. of Hon. Ephraim Hart, m. at Utica, 7 June 1827. SA

Kellog, C. O., and N. B. Baker, of Marcellus, m. at Skaneateles, 26 June 1851. SD

Kellogg, Christopher, of Auburn, and Elizabeth Sherman, of Skaneateles, m. at Skaneateles, 23 Oct. 1838. SC

Kellog, Converse A., of Chicago, son of Augustus Kellogg, of Skaneateles, and Mary Louise, dau. of the late Prof. H. P. Woodworth, m. at Chicago, 26 Apr. 1853. SD

Kellogg, Daniel, and Ellen M., dau. of Thomas Cole, m. at Skaneateles, 29 June 1848. SD

Kellogg, David H. of New York, and Harriet Newell, of Troy, m. 24 July 1851. SC

Kellogg, Dorastus, of Baldwinsville, and Sylvia Coon, of Marcellus, m. in Brockport, 2 Mar. 1831. OR, 16 Mar. [1831]

Kellogg, Rev. Ephraim, of Sheffield, MA, and Lois Bennett, of Auburn, m. 3 May 1841. SC

Kellogg, James, and Mary F., adopted dau. of Horace Hazen, of Skaneateles, m. 28 May 1846. SD

Kellogg, John, of Skaneateles, and Lucy Coburn, of Ithaca, m. at Ithaca, 24 Oct. 1837. SC

Kellogg, Newell A., and Catharine Marsh, both of Fayetteville, m. at Syracuse, 13 Jan. 1853. SD

Kellogg, Theron, and Emily H. Osborn, both of Scott, NY, m. at Scott, 5 Mar. 1846. SC

Kellogg, William J., and Harriet A. Barton, both of Marietta, m. at Middleville, 28 June 1851. SD

Kelly, Freeman, and Mary A. Babcock, both of Jordan, m. at Camillus, 12 Aug. 1845. SC

Kendrick, Dr. Elijah, and Minerva, dau. of Jacob Chamberlain, m. at Elbridge, (24 Aug.) 1820. OR

Kennedy, Henry T., of Manlius, and Julia A. Bangs, of Marcellus, m. at Marcellus, 21 Nov. 1843. SC

Kennedy, James H., of Milan, OH, and Hannah Maria, dau. of Dr. Bildad Beach, m. at Marcellus, 21 Sept. 1841. SC

Kenyon, Job, of Niles, and Adeline Richardson, of Sempronius, m. at Sempronius, 24 Dec. 1850. SD

Kimball, Charles H., of New York, and Elizabeth Ostrander, of Syracuse, m. at Syracuse, 26 Dec. 1853. SD

Kimberly, Eli, and Jane Hutchins, m. at Spafford, 23 July 1838. SC

Kimberly, James, and Sophroney Earll, m. at Onondaga (6 May) 1826. OR

King, Benjamin B., of Scipio, and Helen M., youngest dau. of S. H. Greenman, of Mandana, m. at Mandana, 17 Jan. 1850. SD and SC

King, Obidiah, of Elbridge, and Eliza Jane Stone, of Skaneateles, m. at Elbridge, 14 Dec. 1843. SC

King, Seymour, and Adeline R. Smith, of Otisco, m. at Otisco, -- Dec. 1840. SC

Kinne, Ezra, and Mary Youngs, (b. Ballston, NY; m. 1779; d. Orville, 23 Jan. 1824.) (Youngs Family)
Kinne, Justus H., of Oswego, and Prudence Harris, m. at Geddes, 10 Dec. 1831. OR, 14 Dec. [1831]
Kinney, Curtis L., and Fidelia Clark, m. at Cortland, 16 Aug. 1838. SC
Kinney, Isaac I., of Cattaraugus Co., and Hannah Curtis, of Auburn, m. at Auburn, 4 Feb. 1827. AFP
Kinney, Milton A., editor of the Cortland Observer, and Hannah, dau. of Heman Searl, of Southampton, MA, m. at Homer, 1 Jan. 1827. SA
Kinney, Milton A. editor of the Skaneateles Columbian, and Sophia A., dau. of Deacon Seth Nelson, m. at Cortland, 9 June 1841. SC
Kirkpatrick, Dr. William, and Nancy Dunscomb, both of Salina, m. at Salina, 7 Dec. 1829. OR, 16 Dec. [1829]
Knapp, Daniel C. and Milly Hager, m. at Skaneateles, 9 Sept. 1838. SC
Knapp, Dr. Ephraim L., and Mary, dau. of the late John Sabin, m. at Cumberland, (3 Nov.) 1819. OR
Knapp, Noah, and Tamar Lynes, both of Onondaga, m. at Onondaga, 16 Feb. 1831. OR, 23 Feb. [1831]
Knapp, Walker, and Mary Bedell, m. at Onondaga (7 Oct.) 1822. OR
Knight, Horatio Q., and Nancy Hall, m. at Skaneateles, 27 Oct. 1847. SC
Knower, Edward, of Oswego, and Harriet, dau. of Oliver R. Strong, m. at Onondaga, 26 Sept. 1838. SC
Knowles, Robert W., of Onondaga, and Hester A. Welch, of Marcellus, m. at Marcellus, 15 Jan. 1845. SC

L

Ladue, Isaac, of Onondaga Valley, and Eliza Angel, of Albany, m. at Albany, 28 Mar. 1825. OR
Lake, Delos, of Utica, and Sarah Helen, dau. of the late Thomas Clark, of Sullivan, m. at Manlius (6 Jan.) 1847. OD
Lake, Thomas B. and Nancy Simmons, m. at Syracuse, 22 July, 1827. SA
Lambertson, John S., of Camillus, and Mary Morse, of Syracuse, m. 13 May 1827. SA
Lament, Hiram, of Virgil, and Amanda L. Foote, late of Skaneateles, m. at McLean, 18 Dec. 1849. SD
Lampman, William, and Pamelia Corwin, m. at Elbridge, (30 Apr.) 1831. OR
Lancaster, Joseph, and Elsie Monk, m. at Syracuse, 4 Sept. 1836. SC
Langworthy, Lyman, and Sally Comstock, both of Onondaga, m. at Onondaga 11 Nov. 1830. OR, 17 Nov. [1830]

Lansing, Rev. D. C., of Utica, and Susan Frances, dau. of C. W. VanRanst (?), m. in New York (7 Dec.) 1831. OR

Lansing, Peter, of Greene, and Belinda Wilcox, of Manlius, m. at Manlius (12 Jan.) 1848. OD

Lansing, William J., of Lansingburgh and Alida, dau. of John VanVeghten, of Schaghticoke, NY, m. at Schaghticoke, 29 Sept. 1819. OR

Lasher, John E., of Canaseraga, and Rebecca Cook, m. at Manlius (2 Aug.) 1820. OR

Lathrop, James, of Auburn, and Elizabeth J. Davine, of Scotland, m. in New York, 23 July 1838. SC

Lawrence, Alfred, and Amelia, dau. of Deac. Nicholas Potter, m. at Skaneateles, 21 Jan. 1848. SC

Lawrence, Ariel, of Vernon, ae 80, and Mrs. Asenath Lawrence, of Camillus, ae 79, wid. of the late Col. Bigelow Lawrence, m. at Camillus, 19 Feb. 1823. In 1759, Esq. Lawrence courted her, but went off to the French War, and his elder brother m. her. Ariel Lawrence, Jr., d. in 1807. (No source given.)

Lawrence, Col. Dorastus, of Skaneateles, and Julia A. Cuyler, of Pompey Hill, m. at Pompey Hill, 12 Dec. 1851. SD

Lawrence, Edmund, of Marcellus, and Esther H. Woodford, of Onondaga, m. at Onondaga, -- Sept. 1827. SA

Lawrence, Fernando C., of Skaneateles, and Eliza Jane Cooper, of Sterling, NY, m. 12 Jan. 1841. SC

Lawrence, Henry of Onondaga, and Martha C. Dodge, of Howlett Hill, m. at Syracuse, 24 Apr. 1853. SD

Lawrence, Ichabod, and Alvira Moses, m. 1 Jan. 1832. STJ

Lawrence, Gen. James R., of Syracuse, and Eureka, dau. of the late Horatio G. Spafford, of Albany, m. at Syracuse 10 Aug, 1841.

Lawrence, Thomas, of New York City, and Evalina T., dau. of Walter Weed, of Auburn, m. at Auburn, 5 Jan. 1847. SC

Lawton, David, late of Skaneateles, and Eliza Emeline Drake, of Seneca Falls, m. 17 Sept. 1840. SC

Lawton, John, of Skaneateles, and Sarah, dau. of Joseph Hoxie, m. at Scipio, 23 Dec. 1945. SC

Leach, Col. James S., and Caroline, dau. of Asa White, m. at Cortland, 26 Oct. 1836.. SC

Leach, William M., and Sophia Harlow, m. at Syracuse, 23 Feb. 1831. OR, 2 Mar. [1831]

LeClear, John Spence, of Sennett, and Laura Goodsell, of Whitestown, m. at New York Mills, 7 Oct. 1841. SC

Lee, Benoni, of Skaneateles, and Susan Kellog, of Baldwinsville, m. 6 Apr. 1841. SC

Lee, Seaton, and Harriet Dean., m. 20 Apr. 1836. STJ

LeFeare, Nathaniel, of Skaneateles, and Deidamia Austin, of Moravia, m. 29 Dec. 1847. SC

Legg, Homer M., and Emma Rawling, m. at Skaneateles, 4 Dec. 1878. SFP

Legg, William, and Minerva Prindle, m. at Spafford, 26 Oct. 1837. SC

Leonard, Alfred, Jr., and Sarah Bruce, both of Clay, m. at Oswego, (8 Aug.) 1846. OD
Leonard, David, and Joanna Hannum, m. 14 June 1838. STJ
Leonard, Ezra, and Sarah Adams, m. at Skaneateles, 2 Feb. 1848.
Leonard, Hiram J., of Lafayette, and Sarah C. Lamson, of Arcadia, m. at Arcadia (22 Sept. 1847.) OD
Leonard, Jarvis, of Vienna, and Polly Bishop of Verona, m. at Verona, (23 Apr.) 1820. OR
Leonard Samuel, and Maria Austin, m. at Skaneateles, (24 Nov,) 1819. OR
Leslie, Edmuund N., and Millicent A. Coe, both of Skaneateles, m. at Skaneateles, 16 Sept. 1845. SC
Leverick, Nathan W., and Bethiah Wilkin, both of Otisco, m. at Otisco, 8 Oct. 1839. SC
Lewis, ----, and Nancy Smith, m. at Syracuse (8 Apr.) 1823. OR
Lewis, Eli, and Sarah Davidson, m. in Salina, 12 Dec. 1830. OR, 22 Dec. [1830]
Lewis, Frederick, and Eunice Kelly, m. at Onondaga Valley, -- Nov. 1815. OR
Lewis, J. B. of Syracuse, and S. C., dau. of J. C. Brinkerhoff, of Boston, m. at Utica (29 Dec.) 1846. OD
Lewis, James W., and Ann Curll, of Syracuse, m. at Syracuse, (9 Aug.) 1846. OD
Lewis, John, Jr., and Mary Simmons, both of Skaneateles, m. at Auburn, 16 Nov. 1853. SD
Lewis, Joseph S, of Spafford, and Sarah E. Eddy of Borodino, m. at Borodino, 7 Oct. 1846. SD
Lewis, Sanford, and Alzina Rhoades, m. at Skaneateles, 1 Dec. 1841. SC
Lincoln, Ezra B. and Mary E. Butler, both of Pompey, m. at Syracuse, 24 Feb. 1841. SC
Lindsay, Capt. George F., U.S. Marine Corps, and Margaret, dau. of John Fraser, of Scotland, m. at Boston, 10 Aug. 1852. SD
Lines, David H., and Electa M. Hill, both of Pompey, m. at Delphi (17 Jan.) 1847. OD
Litherland, Rev. Samuel and Mrs. Rebecca Gifford, m. at Skaneateles, 4 May (or 13 June) 1837. STJ
Little, Isaac, of Sennett, and Mary Ann Merrill, of Skaneateles, m. at Skaneateles, 19 Oct. 1840. SC
Little, Capt. William, of Baltimore, and Laura Jane, dau. of Miles Seymour, late of Skaneateles, m. at Battle Creek, MI, 12 June 1844. SC
Livingston, Timothy, of Syracuse, and Adaline C., dau. of Gould Parsons, of Troy, m. in Warren Co., NC, (16 June) 1846. OD
Lockwood, Daniel, and Frances Wheeler, m. at Salina 14 Sept. 1828. SG&GA
Lombard, Nathaniel, and Sally Rowley, m. at Aurelius, (14 June) 1820. OR

Longstreet, Cornelius T., of Syracuse, and Mary L. Barlow, m. 17 May 1837. SW

Longstreet, Cornelius T., and Caroline A. Redfield, dau. of L. H. Redfield, m. at Syracuse, 9 Sept. 1847 (No reference given.)

Longstreet, James, of Onondaga, and Laura Breed, m. in Volney, Oswego Co., NY, 31 Dec. 1829. OR 6 Jan. 1830

Loomis, Daniel, of Canton (Memphis), and Betsey Maria Wheaton, of Salina, m. at Salina, 3 Jan. 1838. SW

Loomis, George, and Almira Pond, m. at Onondaga, 7 Dec. 1831. SC

Loomis, Dr. George S., of Canastota, and Mary A. Lewis, of Manlius, m. 14 Jan. 1830. OR 20 Jan. [1830]

Loomis, Harlin, and Charlotte Baldwin, m. at Pompey, (1 Jan.) 1823. OR

Loomis, Henry, of Pompey, and Submit Cheesebro, of Manlius, m. at Manlius, 19 Dec. 1826. SA

Loomis, Leach A., of Onondaga, and Eliza Jones, of VanBuren, m. at VanBuren, 11 June 1837. SW

Loomis, Nathaniel, and Maria Out, both of Tully, m. at Skaneateles, 2 May 1833. SC

Lord, John, C. and Mary, dau. of Dr. Ebenezer Johnson, m. at Buffalo, 9 Dec. 1836. SC

Losee, Henry, and Almira Beech, m. in Fabius, (27 Jan.) 1830, OR

Losey, Abraham, and Amena Wheeler, m. in Elbridge, 18 Mar. 1846. SC

Loss, Richard E., and Mrs. Brownell, both of Skaneateles, m. at Spafford, 19 July 1856. SD

Loton, John, of Skaneateles, and Eliza Ann Champlin, of Groton, m. at Groton, 9 Fe 1853 SD

Love, Benjamin, and Rosina Sheldon, m. at Auburn, 5 Feb. 1840. SC

Luddington, Liberty, of Salina, and Jane Thompson, m. in Manlius, 17 Mar. 1831. OR 23 Mar. [1831]

Luther, Alfred C. of Lyons, and Sarah Ann Butler, of Syracuse, m. at Syracuse, 1 Jan. 1852. SD

Lyon, Deac. Samuel, of Aurelius, and Alida Cumpston, of Auburn, m. at Auburn, 24 Nov. 1836. SC

Lyon, Elder Philip, and Sarah Smith, m. at Owasco, 28 July 1841. SC

McCammon, William, and Mary, niece of Daniel Dana, m. at Syracuse (5 Oct.) 1847. OD

McConnell, Thomas J., late of Onondaga and Letitia Hume, m. at New York City, 28 Feb. 1828. SA

McCracken, Nathan, and Charlotte Kellogg, m. 4 May 1836. STJ

McDonald, John, and Clementine Fife, both of Auburn, m. at Syracuse, 22 June 1853. SD

McGowan, Harrison W., of Jordan, and Caroline Cornelia, dau. of Harvey Canfield, of Lafayette, m. 23 Aug. 1843. SC

Mack, Ebenezer, editor of the Ithaca American Journal, and Ellenor Dey, m. at Romulus, (9 Feb.)1820. OR

McKay, Frederick, and Louisa Hutchens, both of Spafford, m. at Scott, 8 Oct. 1837. SC

Mackelroy, John, and Emma Atwood, both of Syracuse, m. at Syracuse, (1 Nov.) 1836. OD

McMaster, David, of Bath, NY, and Adaline A. Humphrey, of Marcellus, m. at Marcellus, 16 Feb. 1828. SA

McMillen, Alexander, of Skaneateles, and Mary, dau. of Daniel Copeland, of Cortland, m. at Cortland, 7 June 1843. SC

McNelley, Edward, and Ann Crossland, both of Mottville, m. at Mottville, 18 July 1852, SD

Maine, Andrew, and Tacy Ann Cole, both of Camillus, m. at Syracuse, 1 Feb. 1853. SD

Makyes, Amos, and M. R. Browning, m. at Onondaga, 13 May 1838. SC

Manchester, Elias C., of Scipio, and Mary Ann, dau. of Perry Howland, m. at Ledyard, 1 Jan. 1835. SC

Mann, C. F., and Eliza Follet, both of Troy, m. at Manlius, 23 Sept. 1841. SC

Manter, Dr. H. H., of Otisco, and Amelia C. Clapp, of Syracuse, m. at Syracuse, 13 May 1838. SC

Marble, Stephen K., of Marcellus, and Ann Julia Grennel, m. at Otisco, 20 Oct. 1845. SC

Markham, George of Auburn, and Annie Hopkins, of Skaneateles, m. at Skaneateles, 1 Sept. 1841. SC

Marsh, Caleb P., and Laura S., dau. of James R. Baldridge, m. at Cincinnati, OH, 1 Feb. 1852. SD

Marshall, Arthur, of Genoa, and Nancy J. Francis, of Niles, m. at Skaneateles, 25 Sept. 1849. SD

Marshall, John B., and Caroline P. Cook, of Waterloo, m. at Waterloo, 1 Dec. 1852. SD

Marshall, William, of Auburn, and Sarah Bench, of Sennett, m. at Sennett, 28 Feb. 1839. SC

Martin, David, and Diantha Lewis, m. at Marcellus, 23 Oct. 1827. SA

Martin, Jonathan, of IL, and Amanda Douglass, late of Skaneateles, m. at Jacksonville (IL?), 19 Feb. 1848. SC

Martin, Silas B., of Albany Co., NY, and Harriet L., dau. of David Francis, of Skaneateles, m. at Skaneateles, 26 Jan. 1842. SC

Martin, William A. of Syracuse, and Susan Campbell, of Elbridge, m. at Elbridge, 16 May 1838. SC

Marvin, Edgar, and Elizabeth F. Ashley, both of Syracuse, m. at Syracuse, 23 June 1853. SD

Mason, J. R. and Betsey Ann Hicks, m. at Spafford, 1 Feb. 1844, DC

Masters, Joseph E. of the Syracuse Star, and Eliza Jane Aiken, of Hallowell, ME., m. at Hallowell, 5 June 1850. SD

Mather, Hon. Hiram, of Elbridge, and Mary P., dau. of Dr. Joseph P. Cole, m. in Auburn, (7 Dec.) 1831. OR

Matthews, Samuel R., of Salina, and Betsey Hutchinson, of Onondaga, m. at Onondaga Valley, (1 Jan.) 1826. OR

Maxson, Dr. B., and Emeline Babcock, m. at Scott, 28 Jan. 1838. SC

Maxson, John, of Scott, and Mary Jane Davis, of Spafford, m. 18 Jan. 1848. SC

Meade, Harvey, and Almira Goodrich, m. at Skaneateles, -- Feb. 1826. OR

Meigs, David, and Matilda Bennett, both of Amboy, m. at Elbridge, 23 Nov. 1827. SA

Meldrum, James, and Martha Butterfield, m. at Syracuse, 17 Nov. 1829. OR, 9 Dec. [1829]

Mellin, Alonzo, of Elbridge, and Sophia Hall, of Skaneateles, m. at Skaneateles, 11 June 1844. SC

Meredith, Thomas, of Cayuga Bridge, and Alice Conner of the same place, m. at Auburn, 5 June 1853. SD

Merrell, H. H., of Utica, and Augusta M. Beebe (or Bruce), m. at Syracuse, (14 May) 1826. OR

Merrell, Hiram G., printer, and Julia A. Lawton, m. in Canastota, 11 July 1830. OR, 14 July [1830]

Merriman, Dr. E. G., and Lucretia Gaylord, both of Otisco, m. at Otisco, 12 Nov. 1835. SC

Merriman, Ebenezer C., of Elbridge, and Louisa Coleman, m. at Sodus, (3 Aug.) 1826. OR

Merriman, Noah, and Mary A. Brown, m. at Cicero, 3 Dec. 1839. OR, 16 Dec. [1839]

Merriman, Dr. Titus, and Polly Bowker, m. at Elbridge, -- Jan. 1825. OR

Merritt, James (ae 65) and Charlotte Hillebert (ae 53), of Borodino, m. at Borodino, 6 Sept. 1853. SD

Messenger, Austin, and Sylvia Aylesworth, both of Vesper, m. 9 Mar. 1851. SC

Mickles, Lovel G., late of Onondaga Valley, and Jane Delavan, of Ovid, m. at Ovid, -- Aug. 1825. OR

Mickles, Philo D., and Eliza Anderson, m. at Onondaga Valley, 2 Jan. 1820. OR, 5 Jan. [1820]

Miles, Ezra L., son of Gen. Miles, late of Pompey, and Sally, dau. of Judge Leomonier, of Clay, m. at Clay, 30 Apr. 1828. SA

Miles, Ives N., of Camillus, and Sarah Gridley, of Manlius, m. at Manlius, 2 Apr. 1828. SA

Millen, Cyrus, and Angeline Adams, both of Marcellus, m. at Marcellus Falls, 18 Apr. 1844. SC

Miller, Abijah, and Belinda Denney, both of Manlius, m. at Syracuse, 23 Oct. 1831. OR 26 Oct. [1831]

Miller, Alexander C., and Sarah Elizabeth, dau. of Augustus Fowler, m. at Skaneateles, 2 Feb. 1853. SD

Miller, Norman C., of Auburn, and Jenny Adams, of Lockport, m. at the residence of J. G. Port in Lockport, 8 July 1850. SC also SD

Miller, Warren P., and Lydia M. Ford, both of Syracuse, m. at Auburn, 10 Mar. 1842. SC

Millett, Hiram, of Auburn, and Mehitable Crane, m. 9 Dec. 1818. CP

Mills, George, and Minerva Knapp, both of Marcellus, m. at Borodino, 25 Sept. 1842. SC

Mills, John C., of Marcellus, and Abby J. Harris, of Amber, m. at Skaneateles, 23 Apr. 1844. SC

Mills, Simeon, and Clarinda Humphrey, late of Skaneateles, m. at Canton, CT, -- Jan. 1842. SC

Mitchell, James of New York, and Cornelia C. Colton, of Baldwinsville, m. 11 Oct. 1841. SC

Moffett, Frederick W., of Syracuse, and Ellen M. Gilbert, of MI, m. at Syracuse, (15 Jan.) 1848. OD

Moffitt, Arden, and Lovisa L. M. Ayre, both of Skaneateles, m. at Skaneateles, 27 May 1846. SD

Montayne, A. D., of Towanda, PA, and A. F. Kennedy, of Marcellus, m. at Marcellus, 27 May 1841. SC

Montgomery, G. W., and Elmira Gunn, m. in Onondaga (30 Dec.) 1829. OR

Morehouse, Stephen B., and Lucy Blackmore, both of Jordan, m. at Elbridge, 22 Sept. 1831. SC

Moreland, William, of Auburn, and Mrs. Aurelia Carpenter, of Elbridge, m. at Elbridge, 8 Dec. 1853. SD

Morgan, David, and M. Duvant, both of Onondaga, m. at Onondaga 928 Jan.) 1847. OD

Mosley, Charles W., son of Hon. Daniel Mosley, and Phebe J. Curtis, dau. of Gad Curtis, of Marcellus, m. 2 Feb. 1842. SC

Moseley, Daniel T., and Maria L. Gibbs, m. 11 Oct. 1836 at Skaneateles. SC and also STJ

Moseley, William T., and Angeline L. Heed, both of Onondaga, m. at Onondaga, 30 June 1852. SD

Moss, John, and Betsey, dau. of George Chrisler, of Marcellus. m. at Marcellus, 1 Jan. 1845. SC

Mundy, William, of Lodi, and Elizabeth Conover, of Skaneateles, m. at Skaneateles, 21 Apr. 1835. SC

Munger, Richard of Schroeppel, and Mrs. Huldah Howe, of Mexico, m. at Schroeppel, (1 Mar.) 1848. SD

Munn, Bethuel, and Lovisa Clark, m. at Skaneateles, 21 Nov. 1936. SC

Munn, William, of Clyde, and Julia Clark, of Skaneateles, m. at Skaneateles, 12 Oct. 1842. SC

Munrow, James, and Caroline A., dau. of Ashley Clark, of Elbridge, m. at Elbridge, 8 Dec. 1844. SC

Murray, Edward D., and Mary J. Lynch, m. at Salina, 25 June 1838. SD

N

Nash, Ida D., and Mrs. Hannah A. Foster, m. at Baldwinsville, 9 Oct. 1853. SD

Newcomb, Christopher C., of Cicero, and Maria Eggleston, of Skaneateles, m. 22 Nov. 1840. SC

Newcomb, Dr. D., of Albany, and Caroline N. Hopper, of Onondaga Valley, m. 16 Dec. 1840. SC

Newell, Mortimer, and Barnace Chatfield, both of Skaneateles, m. at Elbridge, 17 Nov. 1853, SD

Newell, William H., of Syracuse, and Mary C. Harrison, of Utica, m. at Utica, (18 Jan.) 1847. OD

Newman, Rufus and Miss Barrass, both of Otisco, m. at Amber, 23 Jan. 1848. SC

Newton, Ezekial, of Groton, and Lydia Campbell, of Cortland, m. at Cortland, 19 Feb. 1839. SC

Newville, Peter, and Anna Farnham, m. at Otisco, Sun. last, -- Sept. 1822. OR, 23 Sept. [1822]

Niles, Dr. Samuel, of Niles, MI, and Jane Helen, youngest dau. of Ira Jerome, of Pompey, m. at Pompey, 13 Nov. 1851. SD

Noble, Linnaeus P., and Harriet A., dau. of Samuel Edwards, of Manlius, m. at Syracuse, 5 Feb. 1828. SA

Northway, Ralph, and Mary Butler, m. at Onondaga Hill, 1 Dec. 1836. SC

Norwood, Alexander H., and Abigail Douglass, m. at Skaneateles, 19 Mar. 1835. SC and STJ

Noyes, Halsey W., and Sarah Cowles, both of Otisco, m. at Otisco, 16 Sept. 1851. SD

Nye, Benjamin, and Miranda Fairman, both of South Marcellus, m. there 3 May 1834. SC

O

O'Fling, Rev. Edmund, and Lydia Jenkins, m. at Lansing, Tompkins Co., NY (1 Oct. 1822). OR

O'Hara, Henry, and Nancy, dau. of John Buckman, (or Bushman?) of Scipio, m. 14 Dec. 1826. AFP

O'Keefe, Henry, and Lucy Curtis, m. at Onondaga, (7 Feb.) 1816. OR

Olmsted, M. J., of IL and Anstrus Case, of Otisco, m. 25 Sept. 1840. SC

O'Rielly, Henry, editor of the Rochester Republican, and Marcia F. Brooks, m. in East Bloomfield, 3 Dec. 1829. OR 16 Dec. [1829]

Osborne, J. W., of Skaneateles, and Ann Henry, of Oriskany, m. at Skaneateles, 7 May 1848. SC

Osmond, John, and Martha Howell, m. at Skaneateles, 8 July 1844. SC

Ostrander, C. W., printer, and Elizabeth D. Cutcliffe, of Syracuse, m. at Syracuse, 4 Feb. 1853. SD

Overton, Joshua, of Antwerp, NY and Emily J. Hoag, of Elbridge, m. at Elbridge, 11 Mar. 1851. SD

Packwood, John, of Skaneateles, and Amanda King, of Sempronius, m. at Sempronius, 1 Mar. 1847. SD and OD

Paige, Jerome, of CT, and Mrs. Nancy D. Griffin, of Skaneateles, m. at Skaneateles, 21 Apr. 1849. SD

Palin, Rufus, of Catskill, and Eliza C. DeWitt, of Onondaga, m. in Onondaga, 29 Sept. 1830. OR, 6 Oct. [1830]

Palmer, Frank, of Skaneateles, and Phebe Cuykendall, m. at Skaneateles, 4 Oct. 1848. SD

Palmer, Dr. Noyes, of Manlius, and Harriet, dau. of Isaac Byron, of Fairfield, NY, m. 1 Mar. 1827. SA

Pardee, Harry, and Fanny Benedict, m. at Skaneateles, (6 Aug.) 1823. OR

Parish, Jonathan, of Camillus, and Mrs. Anna Avery, of Syracuse, m. at Syracuse, 3 Sept. 1837. SW

Parker, James C. of Spafford, and Laura A. Dennis, of Pompey Center, m. at Pompey Center, (12 Jan.) 1848. OD

Parkhurst, Dr. Curtis, of Lawrenceville, PA, and Jane A., dau. of Ambrose Kasson, of Syracuse, m. at Syracuse, 11 Nov. 1830. OR, 17 Nov. [1830]

Parkman, Robert B., of Trumbull Co., OH, and Mrs., Mary Burt, of Onondaga Valley, m. at Onondaga Valley, (24 July) 1823. OR

Parks, Ashley, and Melissa Castle, m. at Orville, -- July 1826. OR

Parmely, Sylvanus, and Losi, dau. of Jacob Cady, of Cortland Co., NY, m. at Skaneateles, 9 Jan. 1834. SC

Parry, Elihu, and Julia A. Hammond, both of Manlius, m. at Syracuse, 23 June 1853. SD

Parsons, Chauncey, of Geneseo, and Wealthy, dau. of Samuel Hitchcock of Cazenovia, m. 29 Oct. 1823. OG

Parsons, David, of Oswego Co., and Catherine Frazer, of Salina, m. 8 July 1840. SC

Parsons, Edwin C., of Worthington, MA, and Julia Armstrong of Camillus, m. at Camillus, (28 Sept.) 1846. OD

Parsons, J. Ives, and Henrietta E. Hewson, both of Auburn, m. at Auburn, 12 Oct. 1842. SC

Parsons, Spencer, of Skaneateles, and Elizabeth Kilborn, m. at New Hartford, 13 Oct. 1836. SC

Patterson, Spencer, of Spafford, and Sarah, youngest dau. of Benjamin Eggleston, m. at Skaneateles, 16 Sept. 1852. SD

Paul, William, and Eliza I. Howe, m. 6 Mar. 1837. STJ

Pavey, Henry, of Waukegan, IL, and Sarah Ann Landsey, of Skaneateles, m. at Skaneateles, 31 July 1852. SD

Pearse, Benjamin, and Mary Jane Griffin, both of Sennett, m. at Skaneateles, 16 Feb. 1840. SC

Peck, Enos, and Eliza Ainslie, m. in Manlius, 17 June 1830. OR, 23 June [1830]

Peck, William, of Jordan, and Fidelia R. Lane, of Borodino, m. at Borodino, 17 Nov. 1835. SC

Pendleton, Lewis, and Maria Frazier, both of Skaneateles, m. at Skaneateles, 12 May 1842. SC

Pepper, Dexter, and Mahala Davis, m. at Syracuse, -- May 1826. OR

Perkins, Edwin E., and Rosette Crosset, both of Jordan, m. at Skaneateles, 26 Sept. 1845. SC

Perrien, Lyman, and Rachel Cuddeback, m. 12 Mar. 1835. STJ

Perry, George W., of Skaneateles, and Frances J. Burrows, of Rome, NY, m. at Rome, -- July 1843. SC

Perry, H. W., and E. Ann Elliott, of Syracuse, m. 10 Feb. 1842. SC

Perry, Henry, and Cornelia B., dau. of Dr. James Fay, m. at Chittenango, -- July 1825. SG

Petheram, Benjamin, of Skaneateles, and Rhoda E. Colwell, of Richfield, m. at Richfield, 6 Oct. 1842. SC

Pettibone, John, and Mary Dowin, both of Springport, m. at Skaneateles, 3 Aug. 1842. SC

Phelps, A. M., and Catharine Frances, dau. of Ezra Galusha, of Preble, m. at Preble, (3 Sept.) 1846. OD

Phelps, Charles H., of New York, and Sophia E. Brooks, of Syracuse, m. at Syracuse, 26 Oct. 1853. SD

Phelps, Joshua, and Nellie Bevier, both of Owasco, m. at Owasco, 7 Oct. 1834. SC

Phelps, Martin J., of Camillus, and Almira Carey, of Syracuse, m. at Syracuse, 10 Sept. 1839. SC

Phelps, William, of Palermo, and Helen Louisa M., dau. of Allen Haydon, of Central Square, m. at Central Square, (25 Feb.) 1847. OD

Phillips, Dr. Erastus B., and Frances M., dau. of Rufus Cossitt, all of Onondaga Hill, m. at Onondaga Hill, 28 Feb. 1844. SC

Phillips, Henry F., and Minerva Delano, of Skaneateles, m. -- Feb. 1840. SC

Phillips, Henry F., and Carolina Matilda, dau. of William Hilliard, of Skaneateles, m. 2 Jan. 1842. SC

Phillips, J. W., and Charlotte Bolton, both of Syracuse, m. 8 Mar. 1842 (or 1845). SC

Phillips, Dr. W., and Louisa L. Legg, both of Aurelius, m. at Skaneateles, 13 Jan. 1846. SC

Phinney, Moses B., and Sally Comstock, of Conquest, m. 10 Dec. 1826. AFP

Pickett, Alpheus, and Affa Laberteux, m. at Skaneateles, 9 Apr. 1843. SC

Pickett, Ami, and Mary Fields, both of Homer, m. at Homer 22 Feb. 1838, SC

Plant, Henry, and Mary B., dau. of Simon B. Chapman, m. at Marcellus, 24 Feb. 1846. SC

Platt, James, and Mrs. Susan K. Auchmuty, m. in Utica (10 Mar.) 1831. OR

Platton, Alexander F., of Albany, and Marion, dau. of Thomas Blanchard, of DeWitt, m. at Kirkville, (4 Feb.) 1847. OD

Pomeroy, Flavius, of Otisco, and Sophronia Clark, of Tully, m. 14 Oct. 1840. SC

Pomeroy, L. S., of Elbridge, and M. A. Elder, of Cortland, m. 23 May 1837. SC

Pomeroy, Lemuel, of Otisco, and Sarah Halle, of Cortland, m. at Cortland, 8 Feb. 1853. SD

Pomeroy, Stephen, Jr., and Lucy Lyon, both of Otisco, m. at Otisco, 21 Jan. 1846. SC

Porter, Dr. E. H., of Skaneateles, and Hannah, dau. of Sylvester Gardner, m. at Manlius, (1 Feb.) 1826. OR

Porter, Leyden, and Harriet J. Herrick, both of Baldwinsville, m. at Baldwinsville, 30 May 1849. SD

Porter, Orson, and Harriet Fox, both of Baldwinsville, m. at Baldwinsville, 7 Sept. 1853. SD

Porter, William, of Jordan, and Ellen Jane, dau. of Hon. Anthony J. Blanchard, of Salem, NY, m. at Plattsburg, NY, 18 July 1838. SC

Porter, William V., son of James Porter, and Abby P., dau. of Capt. N. DeCost, m. 16 Aug. 1842. SC

Porton (or Porter), Manvil, of Scott, and Thankful Loss, of Skaneateles, m. 21 Mar. 1843.

Potter, Elias, and Octavia Burns, both of Marcellus, m. at Skaneateles, 31 Aug. 1843. SC

Potter, Justus M. R., and Minerva Gardner, both of Skaneateles, m. at Otisco, 31 May 1846. SD

Powers, Hon. Cyrus, of Sempronius, and Sally Lawrence, of Ledyard, m. at Lansing, -- Feb. 1826. OR

Powers, Melvin, of Moravia, and Harriet LeBarron, of Sempronius, m. at Skaneateles, 28 Dec. 1853. SD

Powers, T. W. of New York, and Laura Louisa, dau. of R. L. Hess, of Syracuse, m. at Syracuse, 10 Oct. 1837. SW

Pratt, Edward F., of New York, and Irene, dau. of Joseph R. Lawrence, m. at Syracuse, 17 June 1850. SD

Pratt, Francis N., of Center Lisle, and Helen Jane, dau. of Deac. S. French, of Spafford, m. at Spafford, 17 Nov. 1852. SD

Pratt, Varinus, and Lydia Burrell, m. at Syracuse, 8 Apr. 1828. SA

Pratt, William W., son of Luther Pratt, of Skaneateles, and Elizabeth C. Hight, of New York, m. at New York, 12 Nov. 1838. SC

Price, William, and Esther Coburn, m. at Homer, 22 Feb. 1838. SC

Prior, Jesse, and Mrs. Eleanor Lester, m. at Venice, NY, 24 Jan. 1827. AFP

Q

Quick, John F., and Mary Ann Dotay, both of Sennett, m. at Sennett, 16 June 1852. SD

R

Randall, Ezra, and Mary Ann Alvord, m. at Spafford, 15 Aug. 1847. SC
Randall, Nicholas P., and Sibil, dau. of Edward Dyer, of Rutland, VT, m. at Manlius, (14 Feb.) 1823. OR
Randall, Stephen, Jr., of Cortland, and Sarah Haven, of Spafford, m. 21 Nov. 1847. SC
Rathbone, Maj. L., and Juliet Legg, m. at Spafford, 7 Mar. 1841. SC
Rathbun, Charles E. and Emily R. Baker, both of Marcellus, m. 2 Feb. 1848. SC
Rattle, Henry, of Akron, OH, and Sarah M. Hine, of CT, m. at Naugatuck, CT, 16 Apr. 1846. SD
Raymond, Aaron, of Sempronius, and Sarah Bodine, of Owasco, m. at Sempronius, 30 Oct. 1851. SD
Raymond, Elias, and Lucy Jones, m. at Skaneateles, 6 Nov. 1849. SD
Raymond, John, of Skaneateles, and Amelia Knapp, of Jamesville, m. at Jamesville, 10 Sept. 1843. SD
Raymond, L. B., attorney, of Jordan, and Levantia Elnora, dau. of Hon. Seth Chase, m. in Worcester, Otsego Co., NY, 30 Aug. 1831. OR, 14 Sept. [1831]
Raynor, Henry, of Onondaga, and Lucy Maria, dau. of Dr. John Hanchett, of Syracuse, m. 18 Apr. 1828. SA
Raynor, Orrin, and Harriet Bright, of South Onondaga, m. in Syracuse, (16 Jan.) 1848. OD
Raynor, Willet, merchant, and Sophia, dau. of Rev. Caleb Alexander, m. at Onondaga Valley, Thurs. last, -- June 1820. OR 28 June [1820]
Re-che-koune, Young Eagle (Chippewa) and Thayen-de-na-Gah, als., Christine Brandt (Mohawk), both of Canada, m. by Rev. H. Beecher, at Brooklyn, -- Apr., 1851. (no source given.)
Reckard, Fidelia M., of Homer, and John Bosworth, of Ossian, NY, m. at Skaneateles, 4 Mar. 1847. SD and OD
Redway, James, of Otisco, and Maria Hinman, of Syracuse, m. at Syracuse, 7 Sept. 1853. SD
Reed, Hiram, and Cordelia Bishop, of Marcellus, m. 13 May 1840. SD
Reed, Hiram, of Marcellus, and Martha J. Glass, of Elbridge, m. at Elbridge, 6 Oct. 1852. SD
Reed, Silas W., of Auburn, and Euphemia Homes, of Ithaca, m. at Auburn, 4 Jan. 1853. SD

Reynolds, John, of Oswego, and Ellen M. Barber, of VanBuren, m. at VanBuren, 8 Nov. 1853. SD

Rhoades, Benjamin F., of Skaneateles, and Ann E. Foster, of Elbridge, m. at Elbridge, 20 Apr. 1853. SD

Rhoades, Osmond, and Polly, dau. of John Briggs, m. at Skaneateles, (1 Feb.) 1820. OR

Rhoades, Parsons, of Skaneateles, and Armelle P. Fay, of Marcellus, m. at Marcellus, 26 Aug. 1841. SC

Rhodes, Elijah, and Andalucia Gardiner, m. at Manlius, __ Mar. 1818. OR

Rhodes, John J., and Frances Augusta Andrews, m. at Marcellus, 17 May 1842. SC

Rhodes, W. C., and Nancy Loveless, both of Skaneateles, m. at Auburn, (19 Sept.) 1846. OD

Rice, Charles W., and Mary (or Mercy) H. Higgins, m. at Syracuse, (2 May or 2 June) 1845. SC and SD

Rice, Joshua M., and Sally Ann Gidney, m. at Clay, 5 Jan. 1829. SG&GA

Rice, Samuel, of Marcellus, and Abigail G. Lyon, m. at Prattsburg, Steuben Co., NY, (7 Jan.) 1819. OR

Rich, Edward, and Lorette A. Lawrence, m. at Marcellus, 23 Dec. 1836. SC

Richardson, Orson L., and Adelia L. Edwards, both of Sempronius, m. 13 Dec. 1853. SD

Richmond, Hathaway, (b. Taunton, MA, 1772; went to VT and then to Salina; d. at St. Louis, MO in 1821.) m. Rachel Dian, 4 May 1798 [who] d. Salina, 1821). See Richmond family.

Risley, Hamilton D., merchant of Salina, and Minerva Blakesly, m. at Lansingburgh, (7 July) 1825. OR

Robbins, Daniel, of New York, and Matilda Louise, dau. of Russell Frost, of Skaneateles, m. at Skaneateles, (9 Sept.) 1846. SD

Robbins, Thomas B., and Alice H. Brockway, both of Camillus, m. at Camillus, 22 May 1850. SD

Robinson, Edward P., of Bridgeport, CT, and Sophronia Baldwin, of Otisco, m. at Otisco, 25 Sept. 1842. SC

Robinson, John Quincy, and Helen Cornelia, dau. of Daniel Ball, all of Onondaga, m. at Marcellus, 10 Nov. 1851. SD

Robinson, L. D., of Howlett Hill, and S. A. Johnson, of the same place, m. at Syracuse, 12 Jan. 1852. SD

Robinson, Thomas, of Onondaga, and Celestia C., dau. of Parley Howlett, of the same place, m. at Onondaga, 5 Oct. 1841. SC

Robinson, William A., of Pharsalia and Emeline Leach, of Syracuse, m. Syracuse, (12 Mar.) 1826. OR

Roe, Hiram, of Elbridge, and Harriet Auyer, of Camillus, m. at Auburn, 16 Feb. 1853. SD

Rogers, Enos, and Mrs. Mercy Bowen, m. at Sempronius, 8 Dec. 1818. CP

Roosevelt, Samuel, and Mary Hane Horton, m. at Skaneateles, 25 Nov. 1845. SC

Rosser, George, and Esther L. Dyer, m. at Skaneateles, 27 Sept. 1849. SD

Rossiter, John, and Mrs. Ann Dove, both of Skaneateles, m. at Skaneateles, 29 Aug. 1845. SC

Rouge, Silas, and Mary Castle, both of Skaneateles, m. at Camillus, 10 Apr. 1845. SC

Roundy, Charles O., of Spafford, and Nancy A. Burroughs, of Skaneateles, m. at Skaneateles, 26 Oct. 1846. SD

Rowley, Levi, of Corning, and Emily, eldest dau. of R. Farnham, of Elbridge, m. at Elbridge, 14 Sept. 1853. SD

Rudd, David, and Amy Hicks, m. at Lysander, -- 1818. OR

Russell, Hiram, of Chautauqua Co., NY, and Ellen Broadhead, of Owasco, m. at Skaneateles, 5 Oct. 1853. SD

Russell, Samuel H., of Salina, and Lucretia Loveless, of Orville, m. at Orville, -- Apr. 1816. OR

Rust, Elijah C., and Charlotte Brockway, m. at Onondaga, (10 Sept.) 1822. OR

Sabine, Joseph F. and Margaret, dau. of Sen. James R. Lawrence, m. at Syracuse, 6 Feb. 1840. SC

Sackett, G. V., of Seneca Falls, and Harriet Haig, of Aurora, m. at Aurora, (6 Feb.) 1826. OR

Safford, Aaron, and Polly Hatch, of Pompey, m. at Syracuse, 25 Apr. 1827. SA

Sage, Benjamin, and Almina (or Emeline) Cady, m. at Skaneateles, 24 Dec. 1835. SC, also STJ

Sager, Sharon, and Eliza Jeffers, m. at Skaneateles, 4 Oct. --. SC

Samson, Joseph, of New York, and Adele C., dau. of Col. J. W. Livingston, of Skaneateles, m. at Skaneateles, 26 June 1831. SC

Sands, John, and Eliza Bradley, both of Skaneateles, m. at Skaneateles, 20 Aug. 1853. SD

Sanford, Serenus, and Louisa Gardner, m. at Moravia, 7 Mar. 1839. SC

Sawyer, Edmund H., of Easthampton, MA, and Sarah J. Hinckley, m. at Union Springs, -- May 1853. SD

Seeley, Benjamin, of Owasco, and Mary Cross, of Skaneateles, m. at Auburn, 10 July 1851. SD

Seeley, Gideon, of Onondaga, and Caroline Bailey, of Otisco, m. at Otisco, 6 Jan. 1842. SC

Sellon, John, of Groton, and Sophronia C. Hayden, of N.H. (New Haven?), m. at Howlett Hill, 19 Apr. 1849. SD

Sellor, Edward, and Elizabeth Charles, m. 22 Oct. 1826. STJ

Sennett, Judson L., of Sennett, and Jane E. Brackett, of the same place, m. at Auburn, 14 Nov. 1853. SD

Sessions, George W., of MI, and Mary, dau. of Amasa Kneeland, of Spafford, m. at Spafford, 24 Sept. 1839. SC

Seward, Clarence A., of Auburn, and Caroline, dau. of William S. DeZeng, of Geneva, m. at Geneva, 28 Apr. 1851. SD

Seymour, M. M., of Skaneateles, and Almira Hill, of Fenner, m. at Fenner, 7 Oct. 1835. SC

Shallish, Jeremiah, and Mary Balch, both of Skaneateles, m. at that place, 18 Oct. 1853. SD

Shaver, Milton, G. of Niles, and Rachel Kirkpatrick, of Spafford, m. at Spafford, 30 Dec. 1846. SC and OD

Shead, Horatio, and Mabel Fidelia, dau. of Rev. Jabez Chadwick, m. at Camillus, 5 Mar. 1825. SG

Sheldon, Albert R., and Charlotte L. Kenyon, of Sennett, m. 19 Aug. 1851. SD

Sheldon, Allen, of Clay, and Lydia Brown, of Cazenovia, m. at Syracuse, 28 Jan. 1844. SC

Sheldon, Clinton, and Martha Bradley, both of Brutus, m. at Elbridge, 23 July 1842. SC

Sheldon, Daniel, of Cazenovia, and Ann, dau. of Joseph Fletcher, of Tully, m. 4 Dec. 1833. SC

Sheldon, Julius, of Jordan, and Maria, dau. of John Bonta, of Marcellus, m. at Marcellus, 2 Mar. 1842. SC

Sheldon, Samuel, of Skaneateles, and Ann E. Bradburn, of Auburn, m. at Auburn, 14 Dec. 1848. SD

Shepard, Edward (or Edwin), and Sally (or Sarah) Howe, m. at Skaneateles, (19 Jan.) 1831. OR

Sherbrook, Freeman, and Annah Guiteau, both of Salina, m. 25 Jan. 1827. SA

Sherman, David A., and Harriet Grooms, both of Skaneatles, m. at Skaneateles, 30 Sept. 1838. SC

Sherman, DeBlois, of Syracuse, and Phebe, dau. of Benjamin Conkling, of E. Hampton, Long Is., m. -- June 1828. SG&GA

Sherman, Humphrey B., of Rochester, and Julia Edwards, m. at Manlius, 3 Jan. 1831. OR, 19 Jan. [1831]

Sherman, John, of Homer, and Mrs. Emeline Field, widow of Albert Field, of Salina, m. at Onondaga Valley, 14 Jan. 1847. SC

Sherwood, Alonzo, and Lodusky Gardner, both of Otisco, m. at Syracuse, 12 Nov. 1842. SC

Sherwood, George, and Esther Becker, m. at Marcellus, 18 Sept. 1836. SC

Sherwood, Henry, of Sennett, and Sally Ladue, of the same place, m. at Sennett, 4 Feb. 1835. SC

Sherwood, Samuel A., and Lucinda Campbell, m. in LaFayette, 26 Jan. 1830. OR, 10 Feb. [1830]

Sherwood, Thomas, and Betsey Blake, m. in LaFayette, -- Feb. 1826. OR

Shew, John, of Onondaga, and Diadama Henningan, of Manlius, m. at Manlius, 7 Aug. 1816. OG&A

Shields, Capt. Hamilton, U.S.A., and Caroline, dau. of Richard P. Hart, m. at Troy, 10 Feb. 1851. SD

Shove, Henry P., and Nancy Ellis, m. at Onondaga, -- May 1826. OR

Shumway, Moses, A., of Mexico, NY, and Eliza A., dau. of the late Col. Arnold Humphrey, m. at Skaneatles, 13 Apr. 1853. SD

Simpson, Samuel, of Skaneateles, and Margaret Johnson, of Syracuse, m. at Syracuse, 10 Oct. 1843. SC

Slocum, Joseph, of Syracuse, and Margaret Jermaine, of Cambridge, NY, m. -- May 1825. SG

Smith, Charles, and Supply Clark, m. at Cazenovia, 31 Mar. 1823. OG

Smith Charles, of Owasco, and Lydia F. Cuddeback, of Skaneateles, m. at Skaneateles, 5 Oct. 1853. SD

Smith, Charles E., and Rokie Hoxie, m. at Aurora, 19 Feb. 1879. SD

Smith, Dr. George D. and Electa Ellis, m. at Onondaga Hill, (23 Nov.) 1825. OR

Smith, Rev. Henry, of Camden, and Hannah I., dau. of George Huntington, of Rome, m. at Rome, NY (14 Sept.) 1819. OR

Smith, Horace K. and Amanda Burton, m. at Elbridge, (30 Dec.) 1829. OR

Smith, Horatio, and Lucetta, dau. of Jacob Frederick, all of Spafford, , m. at Spafford, 9 June 1850. SD and SC

Smith, James, and Samantha, dau. of George Coon, m. at Skaneateles, 2 Feb. 1835. SC

Smith, James H., of Skaneateles, and Mary Hamiln, of Owasco, m. at Owasco, 10 Mar. 1842. SC

Smith, Jean F., of Auburn, and Sarah Hitchcock, of Skaneateles, m. at Skaneateles, 29 Sept. 1835. SC

Smith, Peleg, ae 68, and Lucy Catherell, ae 21, m. at Camden, ME (29 Sept.) 1819. OR

Smith, Roger, and Hannah Conklin, m. at Onondaga, Wed., last (18 Dec.) 1816. OR 25 Dec. [1816]

Smith, Russ, and Ann Foster, m. at Marcellus, (23 Dec.) 1830. OR

Smith, Sereno, and Cathia Duncan, m. at Marcellus, 29 Mar. 1850. SD

Smith, Silas P., of the Syracuse Journal, and Charlotte Augusta Cole (s), dau. of Dr. L. B. Cole(s), m. at Boston (MA?), 15 May 1851. SD

Smith, Sylvester, and Lydia Duncan, m. at Marcellus, 29 Mar. 1850. SD

Smith, Thomas A., and Charlotte E., dau. of Grove Lawrence, of Syracuse, m. at Syracuse, 19 Feb. 1845. SC

Smith, Vivus W., editor of the *Onondaga Standard*, and Clarissa Caroline, only dau. of the Hon. Jonas Earll, m. at Onondaga, 16 Feb. 1831. OR 23 Feb. [1831]

Smith, William, of Skaneateles, and Louisa M. Dyer, of the same place, m. at Syracuse, 27 June 1846. SD

Smith, William S., of Manlius, and Maria, dau. of C. W. Abeel, of Skaneateles, m. at Skaneateles, 22 May 1851. SD

Snook, John Jr., and Mary K., dau. of C. J. Burnett, m. at Skaneateles, 22 Oct. 1824. SC and STJ
Snook, Richard, and Betsey Kinkaid, of Manlius, m. 10 July 1842. SC
Snyder, William, and Miss Burghdorf, m. at Syracuse, 24 Nov. 1831. OR, 1 Dec. [1830]
Spafford, Charles, of Onondaga Valley, and Mary, dau. of P. King, of the same place, m. at Onondaga Valley, (3 Dec.) 1825. OR
Spafford, George, and Mary, dau. of John Brown, Esq., m. at Brownville, (27 Nov,) 1822. OR
Spaulding, William A., of Syracuse, and Jane A. Ellis, of Onondaga Hill, m. at Onondaga Hill, 18 Apr. 1853. SD
Spencer, David D., editor of the *Ithaca Republican Chronicle*, and Melissa Lord, of Onondaga Valley, m. at Onondaga Valley, (5 May) 1823. OR
Spencer, David H., and Janett Corey, m. at Skaneateles, 3 Aug. 1839. SC
Spencer, Thomas, and Hannah Fish, both of Syracuse, m. at Oswego Falls, 19 Aug. 1834. SG
Sprokes, Joseph and Catherine Conway, both of Skaneateles, m. at Syracuse, 26 Nov. 1848. SD
Squires, Mr., and Electa Lord, both of Syracuse, m. at Syracuse, 16 May 1830. OR, 19 May [1830]
Standart, John L., of Cleveland, OH and Penelope, dau. of George Kennedy, late of Marcellus, m. at Adrian, MI, 5 June 1845. SC
Stansbury, George A., and Mrs. Evalina M. Goodell, of Baldwinsville, m. 24 Aug. 1840. SC
Stebbins, Oren, of Borodino, and Louisa Anderson, of the same place, m. at Borodino, 30 Mar. 1843. SC
Stevens, David, and Mary Fuller, both of DeWitt, m. at Collamer, 5 Oct. 1843. SC
Stevens, Maj. George, of Syracuse, and Mrs. Lydia P. Fitch, of Westerly, RI, m. 13 Oct. 1840. SC
Stevens, William H., of Pompey, and Ann, dau. of Sylvanus Bishop of Oswego, m. 9 Jan. 1839. SD
Stevenson, James, of Mentz, and Mary E. Bidwell, of Montezuma, m. at Auburn, 10 Mar. 1852. SD
Stewart, Chester, m. at Eagle Village in [town of] Manlius the 14th inst. by A. Nims, Esq. to Miss Sarah Ann Manchester. 7 Dec. 1830 MR
Stewart, Gilbert, of Ledyard, and Lydia R. Deyo, of the same place, m. at Ledyard, 16 Feb. 1853. SD
Stewart, Henry Y., of Manlius, and Mrs. Catherine Carpenter, m. at Onondaga Valley, (1 Dec.) 1819. OR
Stewart, Dr. L. L., and Melinda Long, m. at Auburn, (31 Mar) 1830. OR
Stiles, John, of Mentz, and Maryette, dau. of Col. S. Culver, of the same place, m. 22 Feb. 1838. SC
Stockton, Rev. Benjamin B., of Skaneateles, and Olivia, dau. of A. P. Bennett, m. at Auburn, 19 June 1820. OR, 28 June [1820]

Stokes, Capt. James, U.S.A., and Emeline, dau. of R. L. DeZeng, of Skaneateles, m. 18 Aug. 1840. SC

Stone, Anson of Elbridge, and Ann Eliza Cronk, of the same place, m. at Elbridge, 2 Dec. 1849. SD

Stone, DeWitt C., of Onondaga, and Deborah Cuddeback, of Skaneateles, m. at Skaneateles, 23 May 1841. SC

Stone, Nathan and Laura Foot, both of Salina, m. at Salina (22 Feb.) 1826 OR

Story, Stephen, and Huldah Clark, both of Marcellus, m. at Skaneateles, 10 Apr. 1837. SC

Stowe, B. F., and Meriam, dau. of Andrew Henry, of Marcellus, m. at Marcellus, 9 Feb. 1842. SC

Stratton, Alfred, and Elizabeth (or Eliza) Hadox, m. at Onondaga, -- July 1826. OR

Strong, C. E., of Toledo, OH, and Sarah, dau. of the late Gen. Hutchinson, m. at Onondaga Hill, 1 Apr. 1851. SD

Summers, Moses, and Harriet Hunt of Syracuse, m. 4 Sept. 1845. SC

Swan, Col. Charles, of IA and Elizabeth, dau. of Philo Dibble, late of Skaneateles, m. at Marshall, MI -- Oct. 1839. SC

Sweet, Lorenzo A., of Marcellus, and Cornelia A. Bliven, late of Auburn, m. at Cato, 9 Sept. 1844. SC

Sweet, Samuel, and Almira Chasy, m. (7 Jan.) 1819. OR

Swift, Charles H., of Manchester, NY, and Mary E. Garlick, of Skaneateles, m. at Skaneateles, 30 Apr. 1846. SD

Sykes, Hiram, of Hamilton, and Harriet C. Cowles, of Homer, m. at Homer, 22 Feb. 1838. SC

Sykes, Timothy C. (or Sylvester), and Sophronia Hurd, m. at Onondaga Valley, (10) Apr. 1816. [Reference for this is given as "Onondaga Valley" which may have been an error for either the *Onondaga Gazette* or the *Onondaga Register*.)

T

Talmage, Lewis, and Emily Kingsley, m. at Van Buren, 13 June 1850. SD

Talmage, Henry, and Sophia Corwin, m. at Camillus, 7 Jan. 1827. SA

Taylor, A. L., of Onondaga, and A. L. (or L. A.) Dilts, of Skaneateles, m. at Skaneateles, 2 or 7 June, 1850. SD and SC

Taylor, Archibald, of Onondaga, and Matilda Lawrence, m. at Marcellus (13 Jan) 1825. OR

Taylor, Francis, of Manlius, and Sarah L. Beekman, of New York City, m. (20 Oct.) 1819. OR

Taylor, Rev. Hutchins, of MA, and Eliza, dau. of A. P. Nemmett, m. at Auburn 19 June 1820. OR, 28 June [1820]

Taylor, Mahlon C., and Alice Cossitt, m. -- Aug. 1815. OR

Taylor, Nathaniel, and Betsey Devoree, both of Skaneatles, m. at Skaneateles, 26 Dec. 1831. SC

Taylor, Nicholas, and Catherine Helford, m. at Syracuse, 30 Oct. 1839. SC

Tefft, Israel K., merchant of Little Falls, and Frances, dau. of Silas Ames, m. 21 Jan 1840. SR

Terry, Alvah S. of Throopsville, and Mary Maria Loss, of Skaneateles, m. at Skaneateles, 2 July 1850. SD

Terry, A., of Fulton, and Mary Jane Eddy, of Borodino, m. at Borodino, 1 July 1848. SD

Terry, Orren, of New York, and Adaline, dau. of James Hall, m. at Skaneateles, 23 Apr. 1851. SD

Terwilliger, George, of the *Syracuse Journal*, and Matilda B., dau. of John Fowler, of Syracuse, m. at Syracuse, 20 July 1853. SD

Thayer, Joel, of Palmyra, and Juliette, dau. of John Legg, of Skaneateles, m. at Skaneateles, 19 Mar. or 7 May 1835. SC also STJ

Thomas, Joseph, and Laury King, m. at Pompey, (7 Jan.) 1819. OR

Thompson, Addison J., of Skaneateles, and Susan L. Kimball, of the same place, m. at Skaneateles, 17 Feb. 1842. SC

Thompson, Andrew Y., of Jordan, and Susan Gibson, of Syracuse, m. at Syracuse, 22 Jan. 1844. SC

Thompson, Nathan, and Margaret Hutchens, m. at Spafford, 3 Mar. 1836. SC

Thorne, Elias, of Skaneateles, and Mary C., dau. of Joshua Cornell, of Scipio, m. 25 Oct. 1842. SC

Thornton, Capt. William of Genoa, and Clara, dau. of Capt. John Leavenworth, also of Genoa, m. 10 Jan. 1827. AFP

Thorp, Jeremiah, of Onondaga, and Rebecca English of the same place, m. at Onondaga, 2 Dec. 1852. SD

Thurston, W. H., of Marcellus, and Cornelia L. Elsbury, of Skaneateles, m. at Skaneateles, 9 Feb. 1853. SD

Tippits, Charles, and Kate Estelle, dau. of Dr. Hunsiker, of Owasco, m. at Owasco, 23 Feb. 1879. SD

Titus, Horace, of South Onondaga, and Nancy C., dau. of Hiram Gilbert, of Jamesville, m. at Jamesville, (10 Feb.)1847. SD

Titus, Leonard, and Maria V. Baker, m. at Salina, 8 Dec. 1827. SA

Tomlinson, Nelson, of Utica, and Meranda, dau. of Barney Caswell, of Scipio, m. 31 Dec. 1826. AFP

Tompkins, Henry, from near Owasco, and Harriet Garlock, of Skaneateles, m. at Skaneateles, 16 June 1847. SC

Topping, Charles C. of Camillus, and Mrs. Jerusha Bishop, of the same place, m. 4 Aug. 1825. SG

Touslee, Royal E., and Emily, dau. of Samuel Francis, of Skaneateles, m. at Kenosha, WI, 25 Feb. 1851. SD

Tousley, Sylvanus, and Harriet Danforth, m. at Manlius, (1 June) 1818. OR

Town, Isaac, of Spafford, and Hannah Furnace, of Marcellus, m. at Marcellus, 3 Sept. 1835. SC

Townsend, Henry of Auburn, and Lorana LeBarron, of the same place., m. at Auburn, 15 Nov. 1853. SD

Tracy, Hon, S. M., of MN, and Susan A., dau. of Israel Huntington, m. at Syracuse, 24 June 1853. SD

Tucker, Benjamin C. W., of Skaneateles, and Mary Champney, of Rochester, m. 29 June 1840. SC

Turner, Newell, and Laura Cuddeback, m. at Skaneateles, 15 Feb. 1849. SD

Tuttle, Benjamin W., and Polly Leach, m. at Cicero, (16 Mar.) 1831. OR

Tuttle, Elias, lawyer, of Baldwinsville, and Caroline Brockway, of Jeromesville, m. 16 Jan. 1837. SW

Tuttle, John R., of Otisco, and Lucy E., dau. of E. Gambell, of Otisco, m. at Otisco, 24 Dec. 1826. SC

Twogood, Sidney, of Syracuse, and Olive Slade (or Augusta Beebe) of the same place, m. (18 May) 1826. OR

Tyler, James, of Skaneateles, and Maria, dau. of Joel Cluff, of Truxton, m. at Truxton, 1 Nov. 1838. SC

Tyler, Oren, and Elizabeth Longstreet, m. at Onondaga Valley, (1 Jan.) 1828. OR

VanAllen, J. J., of Jefferson, NY, and Sophie L. Downer, of Auburn, m. 21 June 1852. SD

Van Auken, Kelsey, and Rosanna, dau. of William Lowry, late of Skaneateles, m. at Clarkson, NY, 25 Jan. 1844. SC

VanBuren, Daniel, of Fulton, and Louisa J. Hewes, of Baldwinsville, m. -- Dec. 1840. SC

VanBuskirk, John B. of Otisco, and Mary Bowers, of the same place, m. at Otisco, 10 Oct. 1840. SC

VanFleet, Gerritt, of Wolcott, and Harriet Humphrey, of Skaneateles, m. at Skaneateles, 2 Jan. 1848. SD

VanGuilder, Henry, of Marcellus (or Skaneateles), and Mary Loun, of the same place, m. at Sennett, 27 Feb. 1828. SA

VanRensselaer, Dr. Killian, and Amanda Carter, m. at Otisco, (19) Sept. 1818. OR

VanRoozen, Henry, and Sally Lee, m. at Auburn, 4 Oct. 1823. OG

VanSaun, George, of Skaneateles, and Mary Ford, of the same place, m. at Weedsport, 20 May 1849. SD

VanSchaick, Charles, of Sempronius, and Delia Atwater, of the same place, m. at Sempronius, 4 July 1850. SC

VanVleck, J. Dorsey, of Skaneateles, and Louisa Gurnee, of Niles, m. at Auburn, 23 May 1848. SD

VanVleck, Matthew, of Salina, and Maria Fay, of the same place, m. at Salina, (11 Jan.) 1823. OR

VanVranken, Richard, of Borodino, and Rhoda Davis, of the same place, m. at Borodino, 4 Feb. 1852. SD

Vickray, Stephen, of Volney, and Jerusha Gordon, of Clay, m. at Salina, 12 Jan. 1829. SG&GA

Vosburg, Henry, and Patty Kibby, m. at Camillus, -- Mar. 1826. OR

Vosburgh, Peter, and Margaret Lawrence, m. at Albany (29 Mar.) 1815. OR

Vowles, Levi, of Skaneateles, and Jane, dau. of Levi Lee, of Marcellus, m. at Marcellus, 5 July 1842. SC

W

Wadsworth, Horace, of Onondaga, and Sabrina Fields, of the same place, m. at Syracuse, 18 Mar. 1828. SA

Walcott, Rev. Jerimiah, of WI, and Caroline, dau. of Isaac Cooper, of Auburn, m. at Auburn, -- June 1833. SD

Waldron, William, of Paris, NY, and Amelia Colvin, of Skaneateles, m. at Skaneateles, 25 Sept. 1838. SC

Waldrum, Lyman, of Skaneateles, and Rachel Jane Chapman, of the same place, m. at Skaneateles, 5 Nov. 1849. SD

Wallace, Capt. John Porter, of Fabius, and Matilda Hawley, of Camillus, m. at Camillus, 5 Sept. 1827. SA

Walter, Jacob, of Onondaga, and Sarah Clark, m. at Manlius (27 Apr.) 1831. OR

Walworth, Mansfield E., and Ellen, dau. of the late Col. Harding, [Smith? See following entry) of KY, m. at Saratoga, 29 July 1852. SD

Walworth, Reuben H., of Saratoga Springs, and Mrs. Sarah E. Smith, widow of the late Col. Hardin [Smith?], killed at Buena Vista, m. at Harrisburg Springs, KY, 27 Apr. 1851. SD

Ware, Lester, of Skaneateles, and Esther E. Evans, of VanBuren, m. at VanBuren, 3 Mar. 1851. SD

Warne, Elbert, and Jane Ann, dau. of Morehouse Hickok, of Onondaga, m. at Jamesville, 12 Apr. 1831. OR, 27 Apr. [1831]

Warner, Marshall, of VanBuren, and Sally A. Foster, of the same place, m. at VanBuren, 13 May 1852. SD

Warren, Horatio, of Buffalo, and Betsey E. Dodge, of Geddes, m. at Geddes, 2 Dec. 1830. OR, 8 Dec. [1830]

Watson, Charles, son of R. P. Watson, of Skaneateles, and Olive H. Howard, of Elbridge, m. at Elbridge, 23 Sept. 1851. SD

Watson, Stephen, and Hannah Kinyon, both of Onondaga, m. at Skaneateles, 18 Aug. 1842. SC

Weaver, Artemus, and Clarissa Edwards, m. at Skaneateles, (20 Oct.) 1830. OR

Webb, Charles E., and Maria Butler, m. at Pompey, 29 Oct. 1826. SA

Webb, Judson, of Onondaga Hollow, and Betsey Jones, m. at Onondaga West Hill, 19 Oct. 1830. OR, 20 Oct. [1830]

Webb, William, of Elbridge, and Lydia Jane Hall of Waterloo, m. at Waterloo, 7 Nov. 1853. SD

Webster, Hon. Daniel, and Caroline, dau. of H. LeRoy, m. at New York 12 Dec. 1829. OR 6 Jan. 1830

Webster, Prof. Horace of Geneva College, and Sarah M. Fowler, of Albany, m. 27 Mar. 1827. OD

Weeks, Levi, and Eliza, dau. of James Bradford, late of Somersetshire (Eng.?), m. at Skaneateles, 16 Nov. 1842. SD

Weisert, Christian, and Mary Hays, of Mentz, m. at Mottville, 5 Oct. 1851. SD

Weller, Alpheus M., of Skaneateles, and Mary A. S. Benedict, of the same place, m. at Skaneateles, 14 Mar. 1848. SC

Wellington, Lewis, of Skaneateles, and Mary Cottle, of the same place, m. at Skaneateles, 11 Dec. 1853. SD

Wells, Alonzo, of Onondaga, and Matilda Greene of Syracuse, m. at Syracuse, 2 Dec. 1841. SC

Wells, John S., and Polly, dau. of Moses H. Hinsdale, of Pompey, m. 6 Oct. 1828. SG&GA

Wells, Oliver, and Rowana Johnson, m. at Camillus, 7 Jan. 1827. SA

Welsh, Warner H., of Marcellus, and Mareb, dau. of Dr. Bildad Beach, of the same place, m. at Marcellus, 6 June 1843. SC

West, Lewis, and Mary Ann Griffin, m. 26 Dec. 1835. STJ

Westcott, Ira, of Syracuse, and Mary Cone, of Matthew's Mills, m. at Syracuse, (10 Sept.) 1846. OD

Weston, Edward, of Spafford, and Ulyssa Earll, of Marcellus, m. at Marcellus, 21 Mar. 1851. SD

Wethy, Octavius S., of Port Byron, and Josephine E. Lamb, of Skaneateles, m. at Skaneateles, 20 Sept. 1849. SD

Wheadon, George, of Marcellus, and Mercy Jan Barnard, of the same place, m. at Marcellus, 12 Mar. 1845. SC

Wheadon, O. D., of Fulton, son of S. C. Wheadon, and Sarah D., only dau. of Jirah Chase, of Granby, m. at Baldwinsville, 30 Jan. 1853. SD

Wheeler, Samuel, of DeWitt, and Eliza C. Goodrich, of Syracuse, m. at Syracuse, (22 Oct.) 1846. OD

Wheeler, Truman, of Pompey, and Phebe Maria Foot, of Salina, m. at Salina, (9 Feb.) 1826. OR

Wheeler, William R., of Rockford, IL, and Caroline Lawrence, of Skaneateles, m. at Skaneateles, -- Mar. 1853. SD

Whitcomb, James, of Otisco, and Sarah A., dau. of Joseph Clift, of Onondaga, m. 1 Mar. 1841. SC

White, Albert A., of Port Byron, and Susan B. Hill, of Mottville, m. at Auburn, 28 Jan. 1853. SD

White, Alfred, of Auburn, and Sarah M. Booth, of Rochester, m. at Rochester, 8 Jan. 1839. SC

White, Elisha, and Emeline Chapman, m. 4 Mar. 1832. STJ

White, Luna, of Auburn, and Lucretia Bemis, of Spencer, MA, m. 14 Nov. 1826. AFP

White, William A., of Marcellus, and Martha A. Chandler, of the same place, m. at Owasco, 1 Feb. 1852. SD

Whitmore, Jabez K., of Otisco, and Lucy A. Kingsley, of Liverpool, m. 1 June 1853. SD

Whitney, Elisha, merchant of Poughkeepsie, and Helen, dau. of Hon. Joshua Forman, m. at Syracuse, 18 Aug. 1831. OR, 24 Aug. [1831]

Wiard, Newell, and Emily Higley, m. at Onondaga, (7 Oct.) 1822. OR

Wicks, William, from England, and Maria Bronson, from England, m. at Skaneateles, 8 May 1845. SC

Weiting, Dr. J. M. of Syracuse, and Phena M. Brockway, of the same place, m. at Brockport, (20 Sept.) 1846. OD

Wilber, Calvin C., of Camillus, and Caroline Brown, of Scott, m. at Homer, 25 June 1856. OD

Wilbur, Easton, of Syracuse, and Maria Driscoll, of Manlius, m. at Manlius, (29 Dec.) 1825. OR

Wilbur, William H., and Sally Angeline Farmer, of Spafford, , m. at Auburn, 25 Dec. 1844. SC

Wilgus, Nathaniel, and Julia Ann Higgins, m. at Manlius, -- May 1815. OR

Wilkin, Abraham, of Otisco, and Lydia Everetts, of the same place, m. at Otisco, 18 Oct. 1842. SC

Wilkinson, Joab, and Lydia Douglass, m. at Skaneateles, 17 Nov. 1835. SC also STJ

Willets, Benjamin H., of Skaneateles, and Minerva, dau. of the late Jacob Lansing, of Cazenovia, m. at Sullivan, 1 June 1839. SC

Willetts, William J., of New York, and Ann, dau. of Russell Frost, m. at Skaneateles, 23 May 1839. SC

William, Dr. Chauncey (or Clarence), and Bestey, dau. of Joseph S. Cole, m. in Pompey (or LaFayette) (1 Apr.) 1819. OR

Williams, Dr. David, of Mt. Morris, and Catherine Maria Fryer, of Elbridge, m. 16 May 1847. SC

Williams, E. Avery, of Syracuse, and Ann Eliza Bradley, of Salina, m. at Syracuse, 10 Dec. 1849. SD

Williams, Elisha, of Orville, and Eleanor Booth, of the same place, m. at Orville, 19 June 1830. OR, 23 June [1830]

Williams, Franklin, of Palmyra, and Hannah, dau. of Archibald Douglass, m. at Skaneateles, 19 Aug. 1844. SC

Williams, Harvey, of Skaneateles, and Eliza Jane Laberteau, of the same place, m. 25 Dec. 1939. SC

Williams, P. H., of Baldwinsville, and Charlotte Kellogg, of Skaneateles, m. at Skaneateles, 9 Oct. 1841. SC

Willis, Edmund P., of Rochester, NY, and Julia, dau. of Abner Lawton, of Skaneateles, m. 5 June 1845. SC

Wilson, George S., and Mary A. Finn, m. at Auburn, 12 Apr. 1850. SD

Wilson, Harvey, of Auburn, and Charlotte, dau. of Elnathan Keyes, of Penfield, m. 15 Mar. 1838. SC

Wilson, Jacob, of Ulster Co., and Catherine Clearwater, of Owasco, m. at Skaneateles, 27 Jan. 1827. AFP

Wilson, James A., and Henrietta, dau. of Henry I. Brower, of Buffalo, m. (15 Nov.) 1847. OD

Wilson, John H., of Auburn, and Clarissa Dickinson, of Elbridge, m. at Elbridge, -- Apr. 1841. SC
Wiltsie, James, and Hannah Edwards, m. at Marcellus, (27 July) 1831. OR
Winchell, James M., and Elizabeth A., dau. of Hon. N. H. Earll, of Syracuse, m. at Syracuse, 3 Jan. 1851. SD
Winchester, Labonah, and Electa Campbell, m. at Marcellus, (12 July) 1818 OR
Winnegar, Easton, and Ann, dau. of Bennett Adams, of Fabius, m. at Fabius, 16 Dec. 1851. SD
Wood, Samuel B. of Syracuse, and Almira Delano, of Skaneateles, m. at Skaneateles, 28 Aug. 1836. SC
Wood, Thaddeus M., Jr., and Maria Godard, m. (22 Sept) 1819. OR
Wood, William, of Manlius, and Lucillia Avery, of Pompey, m. (9 Sept. 1819. OR
Woodmansee, J. M., of Tully, and Harriet A. Hinman, of Marietta, m. at Marietta, 18 Mar. 1851. SD
Woodruff, George M., of Joliet, IL, and Ann B., dau. of Daniel Gott, of Pompey. m. 25 July 1842. SC
Woodward, Arnold, and Isabella Hayes, m. at Syracuse, 3 Oct. 1827. SA
Woodward, Charles, of Trinity Church, Seneca Falls, and Charlotte Augusta, dau. of Rev. Harry Fitch, of Christ's Church, Shrewsbury, NJ, m. at Shrewsbury, 16 June 1852. SD
Woodworth, A. S., of Elbridge, and Ellen, dau. of the late Edward Bisdee, of Skaneateles, m. at Skaneateles, 27 May 1851. SC and SD
Woodworth, Dr. William M., of Sodus, and Fanny Bisdee, m. at Baldwinsville, 13 Dec. 1853. SD
Woodworth, William, of Mohawk, and Jane Bronson, of Syracuse, m. 17 Feb. 1841. SC
Woolston, Joseph, of Preble, and Alvira (or Almira?) Cummings, of Onondaga, m. at Onondaga, -- Feb. 1835. OR
Worden, Ambrose, S., and Julia A., dau. of R. Keeler, m. at Onondaga Hollow, 18 Jan. 1831. OR, 26 Jan. [1831]
Worden, E., and Elizabeth Cooley, m. at Auburn, 24 Apr. 1853. SD
Worden, Hicks, of Fayetteville, and Eliza, dau. of Benajamin Armington, of Manchester, m. at Palmyra, (19 Jan.) 1847. OD
Worden, Nathaniel, and Catherine Jackson. m. at Onondaga Valley, (17 Oct.) 1822. OR
Worthing, John P., and Martha A. Hotchkiss, m. at Amber, 22 Oct. 1846. SC
Wright, John, of Cato, and Lucinda Langworthy, of the same place, m. at Elbridge, 7 Apr. 1853. SD
Wright, Josiah, merchant of Syracuse, and Celia Bliss of Springfield, MA, m. at Syracuse, 8 Dec. 1831. OR 14 Dec. [1831] and SC
Wright, Lemuel and Polly James, m. at Pompey, (7 Jan.) 1819. OR
Wright, Thomas, and Angelina Knowles, m. at Onondaga, 2 Dec. 1839. SC

Wyckoff, Austin G., and Rebecca, dau. of Deac. Benjamin Eggleston, both of Skaneateles, m. 9 Oct. 1839. SC
Wyckoff, Columbus, and Elizabeth, dau. of Jacob Cuddeback, m. at Skaneateles, 23 May 1848. SD
Wyckoff, James S., of Syracuse, and Henrietta A. M. Beebee, also of Syracuse, m. there 10 Apr. 1827. SA

Y

Yager, Wandell and Jane Irwin, m. at Skaneateles, 8 Oct. 1843. SC
Young, James C. and Chloe Barnes, m. at Onondaga (13 Dec.) 1817, OR
Young, John, Jr. (b. at Ballston, NY, 1777) m. Elizabeth Crossett. See Youngs Family.
Young, William J., of Owasco, and Clarissa M. Doan, of Moravia, m. at Moravia, 19 Feb. 1879. SD
Youngs, Calvin, (b. Orville, 31 Oct.1791) m. Sallie Ketchum. See Youngs Family.
Youngs, Frederick, (b. 20 Jan. 1787, in Ballston, NY - d. 17 Oct. 1855) m. Elizabeth Ketchum. See Youngs Family.
Youngs, James P. (b. Orville, 17 Feb. 1789) m. Zipporah T. Grossett. See Youngs Family.
Youngs, Joseph (b. Ballston, NY, 1781 - d. 6 Aug. 1827) m. Polly Kinne (1786-1853). See Youngs Family
Youngs, Mary (b. at Ballston, NY 1779 - d. at Orville, 23 Jan. 1824. See Kinne, Ezra.
Youngs, Rev. Seth (b. Ballston, NY, 20 June 1784) m. Elizabeth Crossett, Bur. at Orville. See Youngs Family.

MANLIUS, NY OBITUARIES AND MARRIAGES IN EARLY 1800'S

Copied by a unit of the
National Youth Administration

Smith-Cheney Collection, Manlius, NY

Furnished by H. C. Durston,
Village Historian, Manlius, NY

Abbreviations used for names of newspapers:

MT - *Manlius Times*
OH - *Onondaga Herald*
OCR - *Onondaga County Republican*
OR - *Onondaga Republican*
RP - *Manlius Republican*
MR - *Manlius Repository*
OF - *Onondaga Flag*
MS - *Manlius Star*
MWM - *Manlius Weekly Monitor*

Other abbreviations used

ae	- aged
admins.	- administration
Col.	- Colonel
d.	- died
dau.	- daughter
et sequi.	- and the following
m.	- married
inst.	- instant
Rev.	- Reverend/Revolution
ult.	- ultimo
yr.	- year(s)

Standard abbreviations are used for names of states, days of the week and months.

A

Adams, Zopher H., of Pompey, m. at Truxton 24th ult. to Miss Jane Fancher of Truxton. MR 8 Mar. 1831
Alexander, Sylvia, dau. of James Seelay, of Pompey, d. in MI, May 29, 1831. MR 19 July 1831
Allen, Mrs. Abi., wife of Maj. Daniel Allen, d. at Pompey, ae 69 yrs. OF July 11, 1835
Allen, Augustus C., of New York, m. 3 May 1831 to Miss Charlotte C. Baldwin, of Baldwinsville. MR May 3, 1831
Ames, Edwin, m. in Pompey to Miss Caroline Walton, 2 Apr. 1832. MR 10 Apr. 1832
Andrew, Joel, m. in Manlius to Miss Adeline Barnard, 13 Feb. 1822. OCR 20 Feb. 1822
Austin, Mr. ---, of Kirkville, d. of Cholera. MR 14 Aug. 1832
Avery, Cyrus, m. 3rd inst. to Miss Lurinda Jones, both of Pompey. MR 8 Feb. 1831
Avery, Mr. Samuel, of Pompey, m. 3rd inst. to Miss Lucinda Jones, also of Pompey. MR 8 Feb. 1831.
Ayres, George W., of CT, m. at Orville, 24th inst. by Rev. Mr. Fairchild to Miss Esther Norman, of Orville. MR 1 Nov. 1831

B

Bailey, Mrs. ---, consort of Rev. Mr. Bailey, d. at High Bridge (Manlius) 24th inst., ae 60 yrs. MR 27 Sept. 1831
Ball, Daniel, Esq., d. at Marcellus, 26 ult., ae 42 yrs. MR 6 Dec. 1831
Barnum, Mr. Marcus, m. in LaFayette, 1 Jan. 1831, to Miss Elizabeth Lawnsbury. MR 4 Jan. 1831
Batchelder, Thomas, m. in Portsmouth, NH, to Miss Martha Muchmore, 13 Apr. 1831. MR 24 May 1831
Bates, Mr. Henry, of Syracuse, m. in Jamesville, by Rev. Mr. Porter, to Miss Ann Eliza Hammond of the latter place. MR 14 Dec. 1830
Beach, Mr. John, of Fabius, m. in Pompey, 20 Jan. 1831, to Miss Amanda Pease of the latter place. MR 8 Feb. 1831
Beardsley, Morgan L., late of Canandaigua, d. at Cherry Valley, 8th inst. MR 20 Sept. 1831
Beebee, James L., and Miss Alma C. Williams, both of Pompey, m. 12 Jan. 1831. MR 18 Jan. 1831
Bennett, Mr. M., of Pompey, m. in Auburn, on the 16th, to Miss Catharine Beach, of the latter place. MR 22 Feb. 1831
Bennett, Rueben, d. at Manlius, on the lst inst., ae 53 yrs. MR 4 Oct. 1831

Bickford, William, infant son of Col. D. B. Bickford, d. 22nd inst., ae 18 mos. MR 25 Sept. 1832

Bingham, Mr., of Onondaga, m. 28 Sept. to Miss Ruth Lawrence, of Camillus. MR 12 Oct. 1830

Bird, Miles, late of the town of Manlius...Admns. notice. MR 7 June 1831

Bird, Col. Milo, d. at his residence in Manlius 12 Oct. 1830, ae 38 yrs. MR 12 Oct 1830

Birge, Col. John W., m. in Albany, Thurs. morning, 26th ult., to Miss Charlotte A. James of Cazenovia. MR 31 July 1831.

Bishop Edwin, m. at Pompey Hill, 2 June 1831, to Miss Juliann Carlton, of the latter place. MR 2 June 1831

Blake, Joseph R., of the U. S. Navy, d. in the City of Washington, 8 June 1831, ae 25 yrs. MR 14 June 1831

Bloterwick, James, and Miss Matilda Caswell, both of Manlius, m. there on the 23rd inst. by Rev. Mr. Cole. MR 28 Feb. 1832

Boardman, Alvin, of Delphi, and Miss Sally Hawkins, m. 8 Oct. 1832. MR 9 Oct. 1832

Boon, Mr. Joseph, of Salina, and Miss Clarinda Safford, of LaFayette, m. 21 Nov. 1830 by Rev. Mr. Porter, of Jamesville. MR 30 Nov. 1830

Bowly, W., and Miss Elizabeth Davies, both of Syracuse, m. 23rd inst. MR 30 Aug. 1831

Boylston, Edward, Jr., on Committee of Arrangements on 55th Anniversary of American Independence in town of Manlius. Republican, Town of Manlius. MR 28 June 1831.

Boylston, Edward, Jr. His duty to attend polls on election days... MR 25 Oct. 1831

Boylston, Edward, Jr. On Committee of Arrangements, 56th Anniversary of American Independence. MR 9 Oct. 1832

Boylston, Edward, Jr., m. in Manlius, 1 Oct. 1832, to Miss Sophia Miller. MR ---

Bradley, Hervey, son of Mr. Justus Bradley, d. in Colebrook, CT , ae 12 yrs. MR 14 June 1831

Breed, Mr. Barnet M., of Manlius, m. 30 Dec. 1830, in Pompey, to Miss Diadama Hatch. MR 4 Jan. 1831

Brewster, Mary Jane, dau. of Isaac W. Brewster, Esq., d. at Jamesville, on the 19th inst., ae about 6 yrs. MR 28 Aug. 1832

Brewster, William R., of New York, d. in Skaneateles, 14 Sept. 1832, ae 26 yrs. MR 18 Sept. 1832

Briggs, Mr. Ira, d. in Floyd, Oneida Co., 9 Aug., ae 63 yrs. MR 28 Aug. 1832

Bronson, James S., of Oran, m. at that place, by Rev. C. Morton, on the 9th ult., to Sarah K. Bigelow, of the same place. MR 25 Sept. 1832

Brooks, Col. John, d. by drowning, 8 June 1831 [from] on board the schooner, *Humming Bird*. MR 14 June 1831

Brown, Mrs. Lauriana, d. in Manlius, 23rd inst., ae 45 yrs. MR 26 June 1832

Bulkley, Rev. William J., d. at St. Croix, 14 Nov., former missionary in Manlius. MR 15 Mar. 1831

Burr, C. C., Manlius merchant, m. 5 Apr. 1832, to Miss Mary Ann Farr, also of Manlius. MR 10 Apr. 1832

Burr, Joseph F., infant son of C. C. Burr, formerly of this village [Manlius], d. at Pompey, 30 Sept. 1834.

Butler, Mrs. Cintha, d. in Pompey, on the 2nd inst., ae 54 yrs. MR 6 Sept. 1831

Butler, Manley S., m. at Circleville, OH, 12 Feb. 1833, to Miss Abigail Phelps. MR 5 Mar. 1833

Butler, Mr.---, of Pompey, m. there to Miss Electa Foot. MR 28 Feb. 1832

Butler, Samuel, of Onondaga, m. 2 Jan. 1831, to Miss Harriet Hall. MR 18 Jan. 1831

C

Campbell, James, of High Bridge, m. 10 Feb. 1833, to Miss Elizabeth Hodge. MR 13 Feb. 1833

Campbell, Mr. John, m. in Manlius, by Rev. Mr. Gilson, to Miss Laura Stout. MT 27 July 1813. (This newspaper in possession of Mr. E. E. Clemons, North St., Manlius, NY at time of original transcription)

Carr, Mrs.----, d. the 24th inst., ae 95 yrs. MR 22 Feb. 1831

Caswell, David, of Manlius, m. on the 3rd inst. to Miss Jane A. Wells, of Truxton. MR 22 Feb. 1831

Child, Walter B. and Miss Rhoda Dewey, both of Cazenovia, m. on the 8th inst. MR 30 Aug. 1831

Chilton, Hon. Thomas, member of Congress, d. in KY. MR 14 June 1831

Clapp. Mrs. --- , d. in Pompey, 25 Nov. 1830, ae 72 yrs., wife of Paul Clapp. MR 9 Nov. 1830

Clark, Harrison, m. in Syracuse, the 16th inst., to Miss Cornelia Morse. MR 20 Dec. 1831

Clute, Gerardus, of LaFayette, m. 26 May 1831, to Miss Mary Dunham, of Pompey. MR 31 May 1831

Coats, Freeman S., m. in Pompey on the 13th inst., by Rev. James Selkrig, to Miss Polly Messinger. MR 30 Oct. 1832

Cobb, Edmund, of Orville, m. 5 Jan. 1831, to Miss Cornelia Knapp of Onondaga. MR 18 Jan. 1831

Coin, Mr. Sylvester, of Cazenovia, m. in Manlius on the 24th ult. by Rev. C. Morton, to Miss Margaret Spears. MR 31 July 1832

Cole, Henry R.,m. at LaFayette, on the 9th inst. to Miss Vastia Knapp, MR 30 Oct. 1832

Cole, Horace, m. in LaFayette, 27 Nov. 1831, to Miss Lucinda King. MR 17 Jan. 1832

Colinst [sic], William, d. in Manlius, on the 9th inst, ae about 45 yrs. MR 25 Dec. 1932

Colton, Chester W., m. in Manlius on the 9th inst. to Miss Betsey Hamilton, MR 14 Feb 1832

Colton, Mr. Ebenezer, d. in Pompey, Sat., the 28th inst.,ae 77 yrs. MR 31 May 1831

Cooper, Cutler, of Jamesville, m. 22 Mar. 1831, to Miss Mary Hine, of LaFayette. MR 29 Mar. 1831

Cooper, Cutler, d. at Jamesville, 24th inst., ae 23. MR 26 Feb. 1833

Cornell, Elijah B., m. in Manlius on the 15th inst. to Miss Betsey Ann Burdick. MR 20 Dec. 1831

Cornell, Martin, m. in Pompey, 10 Jan. 1831, to Miss Maria Dixon. MR 18 Jan. 1831

Crippen, Mr. B. T., of Ithaca, m. the 7th inst., in Oran, by Rev. A. S. Hollister, to Miss Clarissa Dennis. MR 12 Mar. 1833

Crosby, Mr. Albert, and Miss Clarissa Dennis, both of Oran, m. there, 2 Jan. 1831. MR 4 Jan. 1831

Crosby, Lemuel, of Pompey, m. in Manlius, the 10th inst., by Rev. Mr. Smith, to Miss Isabel Gilmore, MR 11 Sept. 1832

Curtis, Mary A., dau. of Libeus and Esther Curtis, d. in Cazenovia, the 9th inst., ae 13 yrs. MR 17 Apr. 1832

Cuyler, Richard G., formerly of Pompey Hill, d. at his residence in Phelpstown, Ontario Co. [NY] on the 14th inst., ae 33 yrs. MR 1 May 1832

D

Dale, Mr. William, m. in Jamesville, 8 Dec. 1830 by the Rev. Mr. Beardsley, to Mrs. Clarissa Seely, all of that place. MR 21 Dec. 1830

Daniels, George B., of Seneca Falls, m. in that place, on the 2nd inst., to Miss Mary M. Giddings. MR 22 Feb. 1831

Daniel, James B., m. in Nelson, to Miss Lawry Bailey. OCR 30 Jan. 1832

Davenport, Mrs. Elizabeth, consort of Rev. John Davenport of Pompey, departed this life at an advanced age, on the 19th inst. MT 22 May 1810. (Paper in possession of Mr. E. E. Clemons, North St., Manlius, NY at time of transcription.)

Day, Dr. Jonathan, of this village (Manlius), d. in Syracuse on the 18th inst., ae about 34 yrs. MR 21 Aug. 1832

DeLamatter, James, or Oran, m. at Fayetteville, by Rev. James Selkrig, to Miss Mary Coats. MR 18 Sept. 1832

DeLancy, Patrick, d. in Manlius, 14 Sept. 1832, ae about 30 yrs. MR 18 Sept. 1832

DePuy, Jesse Cheesbro, son of Robert DePuy, d. in LaFayette, on Thurs., 10 Dec. 1830, ae 3 yrs. MR 21 Dec. 1830.

Dow, Daniel C., of Manlius, m. in Salina on the 25th inst. to Miss Fanny Barnham, of Salina. MR 7 Dec. 1830

Draper, Mr. ----, m. 4 Apr. 1832, to Wealthy Roberts, ae 66 yrs. MR 10 Apr. 1832

Duguid, Mr. William, m. on the 14th, to Miss Eveline VanBuren, MR 20 Dec. 1831

Dunham, Albert T., and Miss Alvira Sage, both of Chittenango, m. there 25 May 1831. MR 31 May 1831

Dunnels, John F., m. in Manlius, by Rev. Mr. Gilson, to Miss Betsey Stout. MT 27 July 1813

Dyers, Edward G., M. D., of Manlius, m. in Trenton, Wed., the 19th ult., to Miss Ann Eliza Morse. MR 8 Feb. 1831

E

Earl, David, d. at Marcellus on Monday, the 17th inst., ae 66 yrs. Long an inhabitant of that place, he was one of the early settlers of this county [Onondaga]. MT 26 Aug. 1818

Eaton, Harry, of Fayetteville of the firm, Edwards and Eaton, m. the 25th inst. to Miss Emily Edwards of Manlius. MR 30 Aug. 1831

Eaton, Hiram, of Fayetteville, m. Miss Zudah Avery, of Orville. MR 30 Aug. 1831

Edwards, Mrs. Harriet, wife, of the Hon. Samuel L. Edwards, d. in Manlius village, on the 18th inst. , ae 38 yrs. MR 20 Mar. 1832

Edwards, Jerome, m. at Fayetteville, 27 Sept. 1832, to Miss Susan Gifford. MR 9 Oct. 1832

Eighmy, John, m. Miss Elizabeth Hoyt, both of Salina. MR 30 Aug. 1831.

Ely, William, of Pompey, m. 18 Sept. 1832, to Miss Maria Loesa Cline, of Caughnewaga. MR 9 Oct. 1832

Evans, Mr. Asabel, m. 4 Nov. 1830 at the house of R. W. Hodge, of Pompey, by Rev. C. Morton, to Miss Keziah Weld. MR 9 Nov. 1830

Everson, Mr. Hiram, of Manlius, m. on the 19th inst., by Rev. C. Morton, to Miss Fanny Perry. MR 25 Oct. 1831

Everts, Jeremiah, Esq., of Boston, Corresponding Secretary of the American Board of Missions, d. at Charleston, SC on the 10th inst. MR 14 June 1831

F

Farin, William, of LaFayette, m. at Tully on the 20th inst. to Miss Hannah Morse. MR 26 Mar. 1833

Farlin, Miss Sarah, d. in Roxbury, MA, ae 92 yrs. MR 14 June 1831

Farr, Bela. Owned land in Manlius, et sequi. MR 17 Apr. 1832.
Farr, Bela, d. at Norwich, 25 Sept. 1834, ae 51 yrs. MR 7 Oct. 1834
Farr, Mr. Joseph G., of New York, m. at Pompey Hill, Thurs, the 5th inst., by Rev. Mr. Hollister, to Miss Mary Ann Tibbals, dau. of Dr. Daniel Tibbals. MR 10 Jan. 1832
Fay, Samuel, m. in Onondaga Hollow, 30 Sept. 1832, to Miss Calista Wilcox. MR 9 Oct. 1832
Ferry, Mr. Eber, of Manlius, m. at Oaksville, on the 12th inst. to Miss Martha Sherwood. MR 28 Feb. 1832
Fillmore, Ichabod, son of William Fillmore, d. in Manlius on the 21st inst., ae 7 yrs. MR 26 June 1832
Foote, Samuel, m. at Delphi on the 24th of Apr., to Miss Emeline Goodwin. MR 3 May 1831
Ford, Martin M., one of the judges of Onondaga Court of Common Pleas, d. at Syracuse, on the 10th inst. MR 14 Aug. 1832
Foster, Libina, of Kirkville, d. of cholera. MR 7 Aug. 1832
Foster, Samuel, d. of cholera; lived near the High Bridge. MR 25 Sept. 1832
Fox, Britnell, d. in Montville, New London Co. (CT), 2 Dec. 1831, ae 78 yrs. MR 24 Jan. 1832
Francis, Mrs. Anna, wife, of Mr. Samuel Francis, d. at Skaneateles on the 4th inst., ae 50 yrs. MR 14 June 1831
Frost, Mr. Merrick, of Pompey, m. in Pompey on the 10th inst. to Miss Diantha Denio. MR 15 Feb. 1831

Gardner, Miss Dorcasina, d. in Manlius on the 4th inst., ae 23 yrs. MR 7 Aug. 1832
Gardner, Col. William, of this village, ae 69 yrs., d. at Avon Spring, CO MR 13 Sept. 1831.
Gates, Joshua B., and Miss Lucy Ward, both of Pompey, m. 13 June 1831. MR 14 June 1831
Gilbert, Theodosia, dau. of Hiram Gilbert, d. in LaFayette, 2 Nov. 1831, ae 19 yrs. MR 8 Nov. 1831.
Gillespie, William H., son of Dr. Hugh Gillespie, d. in Jamesville, 16 Nov. 1830. MR 23 Nov. 1830
Gillett, Mr. Jacob, m. in Jamesville, 15 Nov. 1830, by Rev. Mr. Beardsley, to Miss Helen Post. MR 13 Nov. 1830
Gilmor, Andrew T., m. at Christ Church, Manlius, to Miss Sophronia Lewis, 16 Sept. 1832. MR 18 Sept. 1832
Goodrich, Elizur, d. at Fayetteville, on the 26th inst. MR 28 Aug. 1832
Goodrich, Mr. Selah, d. in Pompey 14 Dec. 1831. MR 20 Dec. 1831
Gould, Mr. Stephen, for the last few years a resident of Manlius, d. 25 July, at Dover, OH. MR 21 Aug. 1832

Graves, Mr. Alexander, of Manlius, m. 7 Nov. 1830 by Rev. C. Morton, to Miss Lydia Eastman. MR 9 Nov. 1830

Gregory, Mr. Almond, of Manlius, m. in Manlius, by the Rev. Mr. Bates, 20 Sept. to Miss Flora E. Miller. MR 4 Oct. 1831

Gregory, Rev. D. D., of Deposit, Delaware Co. [NY], m. at Skaneateles, the 20th ult. to Miss Sarah S. Rhoades of the latter place. MR 7 Dec. 1830

H

Hamilton, Nancy Maria, dau. of Washington and Mary Hamilton, d. at Jamesville, Jan. 25th, ae 11 mos. MR 8 Feb. 1831

Hamlin, Henry G., m. in Jamesville, 23 Sept., to Miss Mary Elizabeth Hadley of Jamesville. MR 12 Oct. 1830

Hannum, Mr. Spencer, and Miss Abigail Huff, both of Skaneateles, m. 25 Apr. 1832, by Rev. A. S. Hollister. MR 1 May 1832

Hatch, Mr. John, Jr., of Pompey, m. at Fayetteville, on the 14th inst. by Rev. C. Morton, to Miss Polly Jones. MR 15 Nov. 1831

Hibberd, Herman, d. on Sat., the 18th inst. at his residence in Pompey, ae about 25 yrs. OF 25 Apr. 1835

Hicks, Mr. George, m. at Pompey on the 2nd inst. to Miss Polly Jennigs of Pompey. MR 11 Oct. 1831

Hill, Charles R., of Delphi, m. at New Woodstock, on the 30th ult., to Miss Martha Frizell of the latter place. MR 12 Feb. 1833

Hillhouse, Mrs. Sarah, d. in Washington, GA, in the 70th yr. of her age. MR 14 June 1831

Hinley, Mr. Henry, of Salina, m. in Manlius on the 5th, by A. Nims, Esq., to Miss Lucy Shaver of Manlius. MR 7 June 1831

Hoar, Mr. Leonard, m. in Pompey on the 11th inst. to Miss Abbey Whitney. MR 20 Dec. 1831

Hoar, Miss Serapta, d. in Pompey on the 18th inst., ae 20 yrs. MR 27 Dec. 1831

Hollett, Joseph J., m. at Rushville, on Thurs., the 17th Feb., to Miss Sarah Fairbank. MR 22 Feb. 1831

Hopkins, Nathan, of Fayetteville, m. in Orville, 27 Sept. 1832, to Miss Elizabeth Folts, of Orville. MR 9 Oct. 1832

Houghtailing, Mr. Henry G., m. in Jamesville, 23 Nov. 1830, by Rev. M. Porter, to Miss Sally Gilson. MR 23 Nov. 1830

Houghtaling, Hannah, wife of William I. Houghtaling, d. 6 Dec. 1831, ae 67 yrs. MR 20 Dec. 1831

Hoyt, Mr. Jonathan L., of LaFayette, m. at Ithaca, on the 8th inst., Miss Hannah Wisner of the latter place. MR 19 Feb. 1833

Hoyt, Miss Melissa,, d. in LaFayette on the 21st inst., ae 20 yrs. MR 29 Nov. 1831

Hubbard, Abbey, wife of Daniel Hubbard, d. in Manlius, 2nd inst. MR 6 Mar. 1832

Hubbard, Dr. Caleb, of Liverpool, m. at Tully to Miss Lucy Winslow of the latter place. MR 26 Mar. 1833

Hulbert, Hon. John W., d. at Auburn, on 19th inst. MR 25 Oct. 1831

Hunt, Stephen, m. in Onondaga Hollow, to Miss Mary Bailey, 30 Sept. 1832. MR 9 Oct. 1832

Hyde, Mr. Austin, m. in Pompey on the 25th inst., to Miss Laura Parks, both of Pompey. MR 5 Mar. 1833

J

Jackson, Giles, Esq., d. in Tyringham, Berkshire, MA, on the 4th inst., in the 98th yr. of his age. He was b. at Weston, and in early life removed with his father to Tyringham, among the first settlers of that town. MT 22 May 1810

Johnson, Hiram, m. in Tully to Miss Polly Bryan. OCR 30 Jan. 1822

Johnson, Niram E., of Lisle, m. on the 18th inst. to Miss Sally A. Sherman, of Manlius. MR 30 Sept. 1831

Jones, Dr. Hiram, d. the 7th ult. in Ascomack (Accomack?), VA, ae 27...short residence in Manlius. MR 31 Jan. 1832

Judd, Mr. Ansel, d. at Watervale on the 2nd inst., ae 45 yrs. MR 6 Sept. 1831

K

Kean, Aurilla, wife of Ebenezer Kean, d. in Pompey, 28 Dec. 1831. MR 10 Jan. 1832

Kellogg, Mrs. Lydia, late of Colchester, CT, d. in Cazenovia, 15 Dec. 1830, ae 82 yrs. MR 21 Dec. 1830

Kelly, John, of Delphi, m. 22 Sept., inst. to Miss Catharine Ham of the same place. MR 27 Sept. 1831

Ketchum, E. G., of Pompey, m. to Miss Maria E. Philips, of Manlius, 7 Nov 1832. MR 20 Nov. 1832

Keth, James, m. in Oran, 2 Jan. 1831, to Miss Emily Russell. MR 18 Jan. 1831

Kidder, Abel C., m. the 28th inst. by Rev. Charles Smith to Miss Nancy Chamberlain. MR 30 Oct. 1838

Kinney, Mr. Luke, of Syracuse, m. in Manlius, by Rev. Mr. Bates, to Miss Sarah Fine Emeline Stone of Syracuse. 1831

Kirkpatrick, William, d. in Salina on the 2nd inst. MR 4 Sept. 1832

L

Lansing, Col. Gerrit G., d. in Oriskany, ae 71 yrs., an officer of the Revolution. MR 14 June 1831

Ledyard, Youngs, d. in Cazenovia, 29 Mar. 1831. MR 12 Apr. 1821

Liddle, Mr. Moses, of Fayetteville, m. at Orville, on the 1st inst., to Miss Ann Dorinda Wilcox of the latter place. MR 6 Sept. 1831.

Limbrick, Thomas, deceased, of Manlius. MR 30 Aug. 1831

Lincklaen, Col. John, d. 9 Feb. 1822, at Cazenovia, ae 53 yrs. OCR 13 Feb. 1822

Lord, Mr. Alvin, m. Miss Lucy Rogers. OCR 30 Jan. 1822

Lord, Mr. Milton, m. in Pompey to Miss Dorothy Wheelock, 14 Feb. 1822. OCR 20 Feb. 1822

Lusk, Mrs. Susan, d. in Pompey, 15 Jan. 1831. MR 25 Jan. 1831.

M

McBride, George, of Cazenovia, m. 27 Sept. to Miss Lydia Souls of the same place. MR 4 Oct. 1831

McClenthen, Daniel C., m. in this village [Manlius], 31 Oct. 1824, to Miss Annis Bostwick. OR 3 Nov. 1824

McLaren, John, of Manlius, m. in Middlefield, Otsego Co., on 4th inst., to Miss Mary Ann Peake. MR 14 Feb. 1832

McVean, John, editor of the *Canajoharie Telegraph*, d. at Canajoharie, Montgomery Co., 9 June 1831, ae 31 yrs. MR 14 June 1831

Mahon, John, d. in Buffalo, ae 30 yrs. MR 14 June 1831

Maibe, Abram, d. at Hartsville, 4 Feb. 1833, ae 64 yrs. MR 12 Feb. 1833

Mallory, Lyman, m. at Pulaski, 16 Apr. 1835, to Miss Theresa French, of Pulaski. OF 25 Apr. 1835

Manchester, John, m. Miss Alice Manchester on 12th inst. MR 20 Dec. 1831

Marsh, Alvin, d. in Manlius on the 25th ult., ae 59 yrs. MR 1 May 1832

Marsh, Mrs. Harriet, wife of Mr. Lynds Marsh, d. in Pompey, 19th inst., ae 44 yrs. MR 28 Feb. 1832

Marsh, Jacob S., of Jamesville, m. in New Baltimore the 13th inst. to Miss Nancy Houghtaling of the latter place. MR 1 Mar. 1831

Marsh, Mr. Lynds, of Pompey, m. at Watervale (Pompey), the 16th inst. by Rev. James Selkreg, to Miss Emily Patten of Pompey. MR 17 July 1832

Maxfield, Dr. Gilbert B., d. of cholera at Mount Vernon, OH, 8 Oct. last. MR 6 Nov. 1832

Merrick, Mr. ----, m. in Rochester on the 2nd inst. to Miss Leura Hamilton. MR 17 Jan. 1832

Mickle, Mrs. ----, of Kirkville, d. of Cholera. MR 7 Aug. 1832
Miller, Miss Ann Eliza, d. in New York on the 19th June, ae 18 yrs. MR 7 Aug. 1832
Mills, Adolphus, d. in Eagle Village, 23 Jan. 1831. MR 25 Jan. 1831
Mills, Moses, d. at Eagle Village, 23rd inst., ae 85 yrs. MR 26 Oct 1830
Morehouse, ----, infant son of Niram Morehouse, d. in Manlius the 15th inst. ae 18 mos. MR 18 Oct. 1831
Morgan, Leroy, one of the editors of the *Manlius Repository*, m. 10 Sept. 1832, to Miss Elizabeth Slocum, of Delphi. MR 18 Sept. 1832
Morris, Oran, m. in Cazenovia, to Miss Olivia Wheeler. OCR 20 Jan. 1822
Morton, Mr. ----, d. in LaFayette on the 9th inst., ae 75 yrs. MR 17 Jan. 1832
Moseley, Charles E., late of Whitesboro, d. homeward bound from the coast of Brazil. He was the son of Mr. Charles Moseley of Ann Arbor, MI, formerly of this village [Manlius]. MR 13 Sept. 1831
Mosely, Mary Anne, wife of Thomas Mosely, formerly of this village, d. in Pittsfield, MA. MR 20 Dec. 1831
Moultrop, Mr. Moses, of Pompey, soldier of the Revolution, m. in Delphi, to Mrs. Martin. MR 21 Feb. 1832
Mulholland, Major Daniel, d. in Manlius, 5 Apr. 1832, ae 65 yrs. MR 10 Apr. 1832
Murray, Theodore, formerly a resident of Manlius, d. in the city of New York the 11th inst. MR 22 Nov 1831

N

Neuman, Philo, m. 14 Nov. 1832, to Miss Mary Marsh, both of Pompey. MR 27 Nov. 1832
Nims, Asa, in Manlius, 2 Oct. 1835, ae 56 yrs. MS 14 Oct. 1835
Northrup, Col. Rensselear, of Clockville, m. at Watervale, 3 Oct. 1832, to Miss Clarissa Judd, dau. of the late Ansel Judd. MR 9 Oct. 1832
Norton, M. M.., of Lowville, Lewis Co, m. 13 Feb. 1831, at Christ's Church, Manlius, by Rev. S. W. Beardsley, to Miss Mary Jane Cleveland. MR 15 Feb. 1831

O

Otis, Norman, merchant of DeRuyter, m. 30 Aug. 1832, to Miss Samantha Paddock, of Orville. MR 4 Sept. 1832

P

Palmer, Henry D., M. D., of Fayetteville, m. in Chittenango, the 20th ult., to Miss Harriet Cady, of the latter place. MR 5 Mar. 1833

Parker, Mrs. Mary M., wife of Enos Parker, d. in Georgia, VT, on the 9th inst., ae 38 yrs. MR 27 Mar 1832

Parker, William, Jr., of Fayetteville, m. 6 Jan. 1831, to Miss Julia Ann Cobb of Orville. MR 18 Jan. 1831

Parkhurst, Dr. Curtis, of Lawrenceville, PA m. in Syracuse, 11 Nov. 1830, by Rev. Mr. Porter, of Jamesville, to Miss Jane Ann Kasson, of Syracuse. MR 30 Nov. 30

Pearsons, Marcus, m. in Oran, to Miss Almira Dewey, 2 Jan. 1831. MR 18 Jan. 1831

Philips, Rev. John, d. in Lurenburgh Co. [NC], 9 May 1831, at a very advanced age. MR 14 June 1831

Phillips, Amanda, wife of Col. Elijah Phillips, d. in Syracuse, 1 Nov. 1831, ae 42 yrs.; gr.dau. of Gen. Danforth and first white child b. in Onondaga Co. MR 8 Nov. 1831

Phillips, Nathaniel, m. in Manlius, 19th inst. to Miss Adaline Clark. Mr. 25 Oct. 1831. MR 25 Oct. 1831

Phinney, David, d. at Eagle Village, Wed., 29th ult,, ae 76 yrs. Mr. 4 Sept. 1832

Post, John, d. in Jamesville, 6 Dec. 1830, ae 82 yrs. MR 14 Dec. 1830

Potter, Harry, son of Mr. David Potter of Manlius, d. 14th inst., ae 19 yrs. MR 20 Mar. 1832

Pratt, Horatio M., m. 23 Jan. 1822, to Miss Malinda M. Hunter, both of Pompey. OCR 30 Jan. 1822

Prindle, Miss Minerva, d. in Pompey, the 19th inst., ae 24 yrs. OF 25 Apr. 1835

R

Raymond, Mr. Alvin, m. at Hartsville, the 4th inst. to Miss Philura Sweet. MR 11 Oct. 1831

Reals, Godfrey, ae 62 yrs., m. on the 11 Dec. 1831, to Miss ----Phillips, ae 66 yrs. MR 20 Dec. 1831

Reals, Mrs. Mercy, d. in Pompey, 27th ult., ae 66 yrs. MR 5 Mar 1833

Reed, Mrs. ----, d. in Jamesville, 2nd inst. MR 6 Mar. 1832

Rhoades, Mrs. Salome, wife of Joseph Rhoades, of Skaneateles, d. there, 27 May 1835, ae 70 yrs. OF 6 June 1835

Rice, Almira, d. in Pompey, 22 Jan. 1831. MR 25 Jan. 1831

Richards, David, of Manlius, d. 14 Sept. 1832, ae 43 yrs. MR 18 Sept. 1832

Rochester, Col. Nathaniel B., d. in Rochester the 17th inst., ae 80 yrs. MR 31 May 1831

Rochester, Col. Nathaniel...terminated a long and useful life in the village which bears his name. MR 14 June 1831

Rockwell, James O., late editor of the Providence Patriot, formerly a resident of Manlius, d. at Providence [RI], the 4th inst., ae 22 yrs. MR 14 June 1831..

Rogers, Elisha, m. in Manlius by Rev. Mr. Gilson, to Miss Sally Webb. MT 27 July 1813

Rossier, Jane Maria, d. Fri. evening, 22 July 1831, ae 65 yrs., wife of John S. Roulet, of Vevey, Switzerland. MR 26 July 1831

Rowling, John, m. in Manlius on the 2nd inst. to Miss Sally Fox both of Manlius. MR 7 Oct. 1834

Rowling, Joseph, m. in Manlius, by Rev. Mr. Snyder to Miss Delia Caswell, both of Manlius. MR 25 Sept. 1832

Rust, Eliza, d. at Jamesville, 13 Sept. 1832. MR 18 Sept. 1832

Sabin, Joseph, late of New York City, d. at Hamilton, ae 38 yrs. MR 28 Feb. 1832

Safford, Miss ----, d. in Pompey the 17th, ae about 25 yrs. MR 26 Feb. 1833

Safford, Shubael A., d. in Oran, the 25th inst. ae about 30 yrs. MR 5 Mar. 1833

Safford, Thomas D., d. in Pompey, the 14th inst., ae 51 yrs. MR 26 Feb. 1833

St. John, Lewis, of Manlius, m. the 14th inst., to Miss Salley Russell, of Pompey. MR 27 Dec. 1831

Satan, Israel, m. 13 Apr. 1831, in Matilda, NC to Miss Grace Parlor. MR 24 May 1831

Savage, John C., Esq, m. at Fayetteville, the 2nd inst., by Rev. Mr. Smith, to Miss Lois Rhoades, of Fayetteville. MR 7 Oct 1834

Savage, Mrs. Marcia Adaline, wife of Moses B. Savage and dau. of Mrs. Phebe Taylor, d. in Delphi, the 4th inst., ae 25 yrs. MR 8 Mar. 1831

Selkrig, Rev. James, m. in Manlius to Miss Sarah Gunn, both of this place, 27 Jan. 1831. MR 1 Feb. 1831

Seymour, Horace, m. in Manlius the 14th inst., by A. Nims, Esq., to Miss Maria Seymour, both of Manlius. MR 18 Oct. 1831

Sheldon, Amarilla, d. in Pompey, 15 Nov. 1831, ae 20 yr. MR 20 Dec. 1831

Sheldon, Miss Aurilla, d. in Pompey, 15th inst., ae 20 yrs. MR 27 Dec. 1831

Shipman, Dr.. J. O., of Manlius Centre, m. at Cazenovia, to Miss Rachel C. Cousin, of Pitcher, Chenango Co. MR 6 Sept. 1831

Silsby, Dr. Jonathan, d. in Cazenovia, 9 June 1831, ae 44 yrs. MR 14 June 1831,

Simons, ----, son of George Simons, d. in Pompey 12th inst., age 16 yrs. MR 13 Dec. 1831

Simons, George, d. in Manlius the 9th inst., ae 63 yrs. MR 13 Dec. 1831

Slocum, Rev. Philip, m. in Sempronius, 23 Sept. 1832, to Miss Almira Slade. MR 9 Oct. 1832

Slocum, Miss Sophia, d. at Jamesville, Wed., 1 June 1831 ae 19 yrs. MR 7 June 1831

Slote, John, of Fayetteville, m. in Oran, 12 Dec. 1830, to Miss Delany Sixbury. MR 21 Dec. 1830

Smith, Vivius W., m. at Onondaga on Wed., 23 Feb. to Miss Clarissa Caroline Earll. MR 1 Mar. 1831

Smith, William, m. Miss Betsey Chapel. OCR 30 Jan. 1822

Spanenburgh, Catherine, of Kirkville, d. of cholera. MR 28 Aug. 1832

Spanenburgh, Henry, of Kirkville, d. of cholera. MR 28 Aug. 1832

Spencer, Miss Maria, d. at Hinsdale, MA, 13 Dec. 1832, ae 17 yrs. MR 25 Dec. 1832

Stanley, Lewis and Miss Maria Dunlap, both of Cazenovia, m. 16 May 1831. MR 19 July 1831

Stanley, Stilwell, m. at Fayetteville, 23 Sept., inst. by the Rev. A. S. Hollister, to Miss Maria Cadwell, both of Fayetteville. MR 27 Sept. 1831

Stanton, Mrs. ----, wife of N. P. Stanton, formerly of Pompey ...report of death withdrawn. MR 31 July 1831

Starr, Henry, m. at Fayetteville, 31st ult., by Rev. Mr. Smith, of Manlius, to Miss Hannah Goodrich, of the former place. MR 12 Feb. 1833

Starr, Thomas, d. at Fayetteville, the 25th inst., ae 47 yrs. MR 31 May 1831

Stewart, Chester, m. at Eagle Village in Manlius the 1st inst. to Miss Sarah Ann Manchester. MR 7 Dec. 1830

Stillson, Henry G., son of Eli L. and Christiana Stillson, of Jamesville, d. 8th inst. MR 15 Mar. 1831

Sweet, Benjamin, m. at Delphi, 8 Oct. 1832, to Miss Salley Hazelton. MR 9 Oct. 1832

T

Taylor, Nathaniel, m. in Skaneateles, the 26 ult. to Miss Betsey Devorce. MR 3 Jan. 1832

Thompson, Jarvis, d. in Cazenovia, 2 Aug. 1879, ae 81 yrs. MWM 8 Aug. 1879

Thornton, Simeon G., of Marcellus, m. in Marcellus to Miss Lydia Chapman of the same place. MR 1 Mar. 1831

Tibbits, George and Miss Sophronia Butterfield, both of Pompey, m. in Pompey 19th inst. MR 15 Feb. 1831

Tiffany, Helin, of Pompey, m. in LaFayette the 24th inst. to Miss Ann Clute of the latter place. MR 29 Nov. 1831

Tollman, Hiram, of Tully, m. in Fabius, 4 Oct. 1832, to Miss Nancy Howell, of Fabius. MR. 9 Oct. 1832

Trumbull, Judge, d. in Detroit, [MI] ae 81 yrs., author of M'Fingal. MR 14 June 1831

Tryon, Elijah, m. in Manlius the 28th inst., by Rev. Mr. Smith, to Miss Ruth Walker, of Manlius. MR 30 July 1833

Twogood, Richard, of Cazenovia, m. in Manlius, the 25th ult., by Rev. Mr. Beach, to Miss Olive Knapp also of Cazenovia. MR 8 Nov. 1831

V

Vanatter, Miss Catherine, d. in Manlius, the 1st inst., ae 81 yrs. MR 20 Nov. 1832

Van Buren, James, m. in Fabius, to Miss Clarissa Belknap. OCR 30 Jan. 1822

W

Ware, Sylvester, m. in Pompey, the 18th inst., to Miss Harriet Smith, of Pompey. MR 25 Oct. 1831

Watkins, Philander, of Delphi, m. in Fayetteville, the 8th inst., by the Rev. Mr. Adams to Miss Permelia Hovey of the same place. MR 13 Dec. 1831

Watkins, Philander, d. in Pompey, the 16th inst., ae 27 yrs. MR 19 Feb. 1833

Watson, Elizabeth, consort of John Watson, Esq., of Fayetteville, d. 27th inst. MR 1 Nov 1831

Wattles, Hon. James O., formerly a resident of this village, d. at New Harmony, IN 8 Sept. 1833, ae 50 yrs. MR 8 Oct. 1833

Welch, Trueman, and Miss Mary Ann M'Enlear, both of Manlius, m. 2 Dec. 1830. MR 4 Jan. 1831

Western, Dr. Daniel, of Ontario Co. [NY], m. in Pompey, to Miss Ketcham, 24 Jan. 1822. OCR 30 Jan. 1822

Wheaton, Horace, of Pompey, m. at Geddes, the 11th inst., to Miss Helen M. Webb. MR 17 July 1832

Whitbeck, Miss Harriet, of Manlius, d. of consumption, 20 Dec. 1832, ae 21 yrs. MR 25 Dec. 1832

Wilcox, Merritt, of Orville, m. at Fayetteville, the 2nd inst., by Rev. C. Morton, to Miss Naomia Coats of the same place. MR 7 Aug. 1832

Williams, Carpenter, m. in Manlius, the 9th inst., by Elder Lake, to Miss Rosannah B. Howard, of Manlius. MR 12 Mar. 1833

Williams, Charles, of New York City, m. in New York, 8 Dec. 1830. to Miss Catherine Elizabeth Bogert also of New York City. MR 21 Dec. 1830

Williams, Elihu, of Manlius, m. 20 Jan. 1831, to Miss Julia Ann Cleveland, of Pompey. MR 25 Jan. 1831

Williams, Mrs. Persis A., wife of Silas Williams, d. on Sabbath evening last, May 26th, ae 28 yrs. MR 28 May 1833

Williams, Ransom B., m. in Pompey, 12 Jan. 1831, to Miss Susan Beebee. MR 18 Jan. 1831

Wood, Alonzo, of Elbridge, m. at Christ Church, Pompey, by Rev. James Selkrig, to Miss Aurilla Sprague of the latter place. MR 23 Apr. 1833

Wood, Licenus, of DeRuyter, m. 9 June 1831, to Miss Caroline Benedict, of Manlius. MR 14 June 1831

Woodward, ----, m. in Pompey, 16th inst., to Miss Alicia Duguid, both of Pompey. MR 21 Feb. 1832

Worden, Henry, of Pompey Hill, m. at that place, 30th ult., to Miss Orrilla Hobart. MR 7 Oct. 1834

Worden, Hiram, of Manlius, son of James Worden, m. in Pompey, 10 Nov. 1830, by G. L. Taylor, to Miss Julia Walton. MR 16 Nov. 1830

Wright, Charles, m. in Pompey, 23rd inst., by Rev. James Selkrig, to Miss Sophia Hughes, of Pompey. MR 28 May 1833

Y

Yelverton, Mrs. Sally L., wife of A. Yelverton, of Salina, d. at Salina, of cholera, 11 Sept. 1832, ae 43 yrs. MR 18 Sept. 1832

Young, ----, of Orville, d. of cholera. MR 2 Oct. 1832

Young, James A., m. in Manlius, 30 Jan. 1831, to Miss Emily Gurley. MR 1 Feb. 1831

Young, Noah, d. of cholera. MR 25 Sept. 1832

Young, Noah, Report of death withdrawn. MR 2 Oct. 1832

Index

INDEX

Abbott, Anatha E. 29
  Louisa A. 29
  Rebecca Jane 33
Abeel, C. W. 60
  Maria 60
Adams, --- (Rev. Mr.) 85
  Alina 13
  Angeline 50
  Ann 68
  Bennett 68
  Jenny 51
  Sarah 18, 47
  Waty 24
Aiken, Eliza Jane 49
Ainsley, Nancy 28
Ainslie, Eliza 54
Aldrich, Angeline 26
Alexander, Caleb 56
  Sophia 56
Allen, Aaron 7
  Betsey 32
  Daniel 72
  Harriet R. 7
  James S. 31
  Judith 31
  Lydia 31
  Sarah M. 22
Allis, Mary L. 34
Almy, Caroline 3
Alvord, Lucy E. 35
  Mary Ann 56
Ames, Frances 63
  Silas 63
Anderson, Eliza 50
  Grace 36
  Louisa 61
Andrews, Frances Augusta 57
  Polly 35
  Violet 2
Angel, Eliza 45
Armington, Benjamin 68
  Eliza 68

Armstrong, Emeline 43
  Jabin 43
  Julia 53
  Louisa 1
Arnold, Lydia 18
Ashley, Elizabeth F. 49
Atwater, Clarissa 6
  Delia 64
Atwood, Emma 49
Auchmuty, Susan K. 55
Aumock, Hannah 43
Austin, Deidamia 46
  E. E. 35
  Elizabeth 4
  Maria 47
  Rebecca P. 33
Auyer, Harriet 57
Avery, Anna 53
  Lucilla 68
  Zudah 76
Axtell, Alva Jen 22
Aylesworth, Sylvia 50
Ayre, Lovisa L. M. 51

Babcock, Caroline S. 26
  Emeline 50
  Mary A. 44
  Silas 26
Backus, Harriet C. 15
Bacon, Miriam S. 14
  Sarah 21
Badgley, Catharine 27
Bailey, --- (Rev. Mr.) 72
  Caroline 58
  Eliza 16
  Florilla 4
  Lawry 75
  Mary 79
Baker, Adelphia D. 33
  Betsey C. 24
  Brayton 8
  Emily R. 56

Baker, Erastus 8, 24
  Frances 8
  Francis 24
  M. Orinda 8
  Maria V. 63
  Minerva 40
  N. B. 44
  Rachel 5
Balch, Catharine 38
  Mary 59
Baldridge, James R. 49
  Laura S. 49
Baldwin, Charlotte 48
  Charlotte C. 72
  Delia 39
  Sophronia 57
Ball, Daniel 57
  Frances Fidelia 5
  Helen Cornelia 57
  Julia A. 31
  Samuel 5
Bangs, Julia A. 44
Barber, Elizabeth C. 29
  Ellen M. 57
  Elvenah M. 37
  Jedidiah 37
  Joseph 29
  Lucy 26
  Susan 4
Barbour, Phebe 42
Barlow, Mary L. 48
Barnard, Adeline 72
  Mercy Jan 66
Barnes, Chloe 69
Barnham, Fanny 76
Barrass, --- (Miss) 52
Barton, Harriet A. 44
Bascom, Silas 6
Bates, --- (Rev. Mr.) 78, 79
  Esther 17
  Joshua 13
Bayles, Caroline 42
Beach, --- (Rev. Mr.) 85
  Bildad 44, 66
  Catharine 72
  Hannah Maria 44
  Huldah A. 24
  Mareb 66
Beardslee, Mary 38

Beardsley, --- (Rev. Mr.) 75, 77
  S. W. 81
Becker, Esther 59
Bedell, Harriet 4
  Lewis 4
  Mary 45
  Sarah M. 4
Beebe, Augusta 64
  Augusta M. 50
  Henrietta A. M. 69
  Mary M. 12
  Susan 15
Beebee, Susan 86
Beech, Almira 48
Beecher, H. 56
Beekman, Sarah L. 62
Beeman, Sarah M. 32
Belieu, Elizabeth 14
Belknap, Clarissa 85
Bemis, Lucretia 66
Bench, Sarah 49
Benedict, Caroline 86
  Eli 28, 34
  Emeline 23
  Fanny 53
  Lodema 28
  Lydia 34
  Mary A. S. 66
Bennett, A. P. 61
  Lois 44
  Maranda 20
  Martha 40
  Mary Ann 37
  Mary M. 6
  Matilda 50
  Olivia 61
  Thomas 37
Benson, Alanson 29
  Cornelia H. 24
  Maria 29
Bentliff, Caroline 39
Bessey, Caroline 15
Betts, Chauncey 16
  Eliza 39
  Harriet M. 16
  Julia 8
Bevier, Nellie 54
Bickford, D. B. 17, 73

Bickford, Mary M. 17
Bicknell, Sarah 15
Bidwell, Mary E. 61
Bienrjice, --- (Col.) 35
  Ariyet 35
Bigelow, Olive 34
  Otis 34
  Sarah K. 73
Billings, Rogers 26
  Sarah Cornelia 26
Binning, Sarah 4
Bird, Almira 34
Bisdee, Edward 68
  Ellen 68
  Fanny 68
Bishop, Ann 61
  Caroline 18
  Cordelia 56
  Henrietta 22
  Jerusha 63
  Polly 47
  Sylvanus 61
Bissell, Josiah 37
  Sarah W. 37
Blackhurst, Ellen 17
Blackmore, Lucy 51
Blake, Betsey 59
Blakeley, S. A. (Miss) 40
Blakesly, Minerva 57
  Polly 25
Blanchard, Anthony J. 55
  Ellen Jane 55
  Marion 55
  Thomas 55
Blawveat, Eliza 22
Bliss, Alexander 29
  Celia 68
  Elizabeth 29
Bliven, Cornelia A. 62
Blossom, Ezra 39
  Lucinda 39
Bodine, Sarah 56
Bogert, Catherine Elizabeth 86
Boies, Harriet E. 22
Bolles, Mary 9
Bolton, Charlotte 54
Bonta, John 59
  Maria 59

Booth, Eleanor 67
  Sarah M. 66
Bostwick, Annis 80
  Philura 17
  William 17
Bosworth, John 56
Bowen, Mercy 57
Bowers, Mary 64
Bowker, Polly 50
Bowman, J. 23
Boynton, Lydia A. 41
Brackett, Jane E. 58
  Lucy 39
Bradburn, Ann E. 59
Bradford, Eliza 66
  James 66
Bradley, Amanda 41
  Ann Eliza 67
  Eliza 58
  Elpha R. 1
  Joel 22
  Justus 73
  Martha 59
  Mary 22
  Mary J. 14
Brainard, Lydia 12
Brandt, Christine 56
Breed, Laura 48
Breese, Arthur 33
  Catherine W. 33
Brenenstuhl, Rosania F. 28
Brewster, Isaac W. 73
Briggs, John 57
  Polly 57
Bright, Harriet 56
Brill, Ann M. 40
Brinckerhoff, Marian 3
Brinkerhoff, J. C. 47
  John I. 18
  Maria 18
  S. C. (Miss) 47
Britton, Polly 28
Broadhead, Ellen 58
Brockway, Alice H. 57
  Caroline 64
  Charlotte 58
  Phena M. 67
Bronson, Jane 68
  Maria 67

Brooks, Liana 6
 Marcia F. 52
 Sophia E. 54
Brosby, Betsey 26
Brower, Cecilia W. 22
 Henrietta 67
 Henry I. 67
 Henry J. 22
Brown, Alicia 6
 Almira 39
 Caroline 67
 Elizabeth 24
 Emily 21
 Harriet 8
 Harriet M. 24
 Jane Tyler 27
 John 61
 Lydia 59
 Mary 61
 Mary A. 50
 Nancy 40
 Susan M. 42
 William 42
Brownell, --- (Mrs.) 48
Browning, M. R. 49
Bruce, Augusta M. 50
 Sarah 47
Bryan, Polly 79
Buck, Evalina 8
Buckle, Adeline G. 36
 Charles J. 36
Buckman, John 52
 Nancy 52
Budick, Betsey Ann 75
Bulfinch, Joseph 30
Bump, Angenetta 26
Burdick, Betsey Ann 19
 Josephine 37
 Luraina M. 11
Burghdorf, --- (Miss) 61
Burnett, C. J. 61
 Mary K. 61
Burnham, Fanny 24
 Sarah Ann 22
Burns, Maria 34
 Octavia 55
Burr, C. C. 74
Burrell, Lydia 55
Burroughs, Nancy A. 58

Burrows, Frances J. 54
Burt, Aaron 2
 Elizabeth 8
 Lucy T. 2
 Mary 3, 53
 Mary S. 22
Burton, Amanda 60
 Avis 25
 Phebe J. 22
Bush, Mary J. 40
Butin, Sarah M. 23
Butler, Maria 65
 Mary 52
 Mary E. 47
 Sarah Ann 48
Butterfield, Martha 50
 Sophronia 84
Butts, Horace 10
 Mary 10
Bylington, Belinda 10
Byron, Harriet 53
 Isaac 53

Cadwell, Maria 84
 Sally 38
Cady, Almina 58
 Emeline 58
 Harriet 82
 Jacob 53
 Losi 53
 Sophia 29
Caldwell, Cornelia H. (R.) 18
Calkins, Phebe Ann 1
Camp, Clark 33
 Mary 33
Campbell, Catharine 27
 Electa 68
 Lucinda 59
 Lydia 52
 Susan 49
Canfield, Amanda M. 40
 Ann B. 38
 Caroline Cornelia 49
 Harvey 49
 Joel 40
 Nancy 20

Canfield, Sally J. 5
Caple, Maria 43
Carey, Almira 54
Carlton, Juliann 73
Carpenter, Aurelia 51
  Catherine 61
  Ruthala 1
Carperat, Eliza M. 11
Carrington, Ann 34
  Sarah 5
  Susan T. 2
Carruth, Lovina 3
Carter, Amanda 64
Case, Anstrus 52
  Mehitable 11
Casell, Charlotte 40
Castle, Mary 58
  Melissa 53
Caswell, Barney 63
  Delia 83
  Matilda 73
  Meranda 63
Catherell, Lucy 60
Chadwick, Jabez 59
  Mabel Fidelia 59
Chamberlain, Jacob 44
  Minerva 44
  Nancy 79
  Sally 42
Champlin, Eliza Ann 48
Champney, Mary 64
Chandler, Martha A. 66
  Susan 9
Chapel, Betsey 84
Chapman, --- (Dr.) 28
  --- (Mrs.) 28
  Emeline 66
  Louisa A. 28
  Lydia 84
  Mary B. 55
  Rachel Jane 65
  Simon B. 55
Chappell, Celia 42
  James 42
Charles, Elizabeth 58
Chase, Jirah 66
  Levantia Elnora 56
  Lucena 3
  M. 3

Chase, Rosaline H. 39
  Sarah D. 66
  Seth 56
Chasy, Almira 62
Chatfield, Barnace 52
  L. 36
Cheesebro, Submit 48
Chidney, Sarah T. 39
Chidsey, Sarah T. 39
Chittenden, Adreste (Areste) 16
  Julia 15
Chrisler, Betsey 51
  George 51
Christler, George 42
  Rebecca Ann 42
Chubbuck, Emily A. 43
Church, Abby 37
  Mather B. 37
Cisco, Caroline 23
Clapp, Amelia C. 49
  Paul 74
Clark, Adaline 82
  Ashley 51
  Caroline A. 51
  Clarissa 39
  Deodatus 10
  Eliza 28
  Fidelia 45
  Harriet 31
  Huldah 62
  Jane 14
  Julia 10, 51
  Laura G. 24
  Lovisa 51
  Maria 26
  Mary Elizabeth 35
  Nancy Fiedlia 19
  Nathan 26
  Sarah 65
  Sarah Helen 45
  Sophronia 55
  Supply 60
  Thomas 45
  William 35
Clarke, Polly 24
Clearwater, Catherine 67
Clemons, Sally 37
Cleveland, Francesca 35

Cleveland, Julia Ann 86
  Martha 2
  Mary Jane 81
  P. P. 35
Clift, Helen E. 1
  Joseph 66
  Sarah A. 66
  William 1
Cline, Maria Loesa 76
Cluff, Joel 64
  Maria 64
Clute, Ann 85
Coates, Abigail B. 31
Coats, Mary 75
  Naomia 85
Cobb, Ebenezer 39
  Henrietta G. 39
  Julia Ann 82
Coburn, Esther 55
  Lucy 44
Coe, Hannah 22
  Millicent A. 47
Cogswell, Ann 11
  Sarah 31
Colanbrauer, Mary 30
Cole, --- (Rev. Mr.) 73
  Betsey 67
  Elizabeth 4
  Ellen M. 44
  Harmon 43
  Jane 27
  Joseph P. 50
  Joseph S. 67
  Laura E. 43
  Mary P. 50
  Sarah H. 21
  Sophronia 24
  Tacy Ann 49
  Thomas 44
Cole(s), Charlotte Augusta 60
  L. B. 60
Coleman, Louisa 50
Colson, J. G. 42
Colton, Calista 33
  Cornelia C. 51
Colvin, Adeline 36
  Amelia 65
Colwell, Rhoda E. 54
Comins, Prudence G. 14

Comstock, Adeline T. 12
  B. F. 12
  Jude 4
  Polly 4
  Sally 45, 54
Cone, Mary 66
  Rebecca 1
Conklin, Hannah 60
Conkling, Alfred 20
  Benjamin 59
  Eliza 20
  Phebe 59
Conner, Alice 50
  Frances L. 38
Conover, Elizabeth 51
Converse, Elizabeth 12
Conway, Catherine 61
Cook, B. W. 28
  Caroline P. 49
  Elsey Ann 31
  Fanny 42
  Laura L. 28
  Nancy 21
  Narcissa 7
  Rebecca 46
Cooley, Elizabeth 68
Coon, George 26, 60
  Harriet 26
  Mary Ann 26
  Samantha 60
  Sylvia 44
  Ursula 32
Cooper, Caroline 65
  Eliza Jane 46
  Isaac 65
  Susan 11
Copeland, Daniel 49
  Mary 49
Copp, Lovina 19
  Melvina 3
  Thomas 3
Corey, Janett 61
Cornell, Betsey 19
  Joshua 63
  Mary C. 63
Cortright, Polly 35
Corwin, Pamelia 45
  Sophia 62
Cossitt, Alice 62

Cossitt, Frances M. 54
 Rufus 54
Cottle, Mary 66
Cotton, Calista 33
 Elizabeth 28
Cousin, Rachel C. 83
Cowles, Harriet C. 62
 Sarah 52
Cox, Mahala 35
 Mary 42
 Ruth Adella 29
 Silas 29
Cramer, Betsey 42
 Sarah A. 4
Crandall, Asenath 20
 Laura 6
 Martha A. 7
Crane, Mary A. 10
 Mehitable 51
Crawford, Julia 41
 W. A. 41
Creed, Helen 12
 John B. 12
Crippen, Frances 39
Cronk, Ann Eliza 62
Cropsey, Eliza Ann 20
Crosby, Elisha 2
 Polly 35
 Rebecca 2
Cross, Mary 58
Crosset, Rosette 54
Crossett, Elizabeth 69
Crossland, Ann 49
Croswell, Edwin 34
 Juliet Eulen 34
Crout, Caroline 2
Cuddeback, Deborah 62
 Elizabeth 13, 69
 Hannah 4
 Henrietta 39
 J. C. 7
 Jacob 15, 69
 Jane 15
 Laura 64
 Lydia F. 60
 Malvina E. 7
 Margaret 9
 Rachel 54
 Sally Ann 37

Cuddeback, Sarah A. 37
Culver, Maryette 61
 S. 61
 Salome 11
Cummings, Almira 68
 Alvira 68
Cumpston, Alida 48
Curll, Ann 47
Curtis, Elsie 7
 Esther 75
 Eugenia 18
 Gad 51
 Hannah 45
 John 10
 Libeus 75
 Lucy 52
 Olive Mary 10
 Phebe J. 51
Cushing, Hannah 20
Cushman, Elizabeth 11
Cutliffe, Elizabeth D. 53
Cuykendall, Charity 35
 Moses 35
 Nelson 35
 Phebe 53
Cuyler, Jane M. 29
 Julia A. 46
 Mary L. 24

Dallman, Drusilla 26
Dana, Mary 48
Danforth, --- (Gen.) 82
 Harriet 63
Daniel, Dana 48
Daniels, Emily 31
Darby, Fannie E. 30
Davenport, John 75
Davey, Henrietta 42
David, Caroline 5
Davidson, Sarah 47
Davies, Elizabeth 73
Davine, Elizabeth J. 46
Davis, Cornelia I. 20
 Elizabeth 37
 Emily 24

Davis, Hannah 22
  Harriet A. 37
  Horace 15
  Mahala 54
  Mary 15
  Mary Jane 50
  Munn 20
  Rhoda 64
  Richard 37
Day, Cora 26
Dean, Charlotte 3
  Harriet 46
Deckerman, Harriet 40
DeCost, --- (Capt.) 10
  Abby P. 55
  Eliza 13
  N. 55
  Pamela 10
DeHart, Marty Martz 8
DeLancey, Margaret Monroe 29
DeLancy, Bishop 29
Delano, Almira 68
  Howard 40
  Joanna E. 30
  Martha Ann 21
  Mary 40
  Minerva 54
Delavan, Jane 50
DeLine, Emeline 17
Denio, Diantha 77
Denney, Belinda 50
Dennigan, Diademia 1
Dennis, Clarissa 20, 75
  Laura A. 53
  Sarah M. 8
Depew, Christina J. 10
  John 10
DePuy, Robert 75
DeVoe, Cornelia 5
  Elijah 5
Devorce, Betsey 84
Devoree, Betsey 62
DeWaters, Mahala 33
Dewey, Almira 82
  Rhoda 74
DeWitt, Eliza C. 53
  Susan 37
Dey, Ellenor 49

Deyo, Lydia R. 61
DeZeng, Caroline 59
  Emeline 62
  R. L. 62
  William S. 59
Dian, Richel 57
Dibble, Elizabeth 62
  Philo 62
Dickenson, Almira 9
Dickinson, Clarissa 68
Dills, Sarah C. 19
Dilts, A. L. 62
  L. A. 62
  Mary 13
Dings, Nancy 43
Dixon, Maria 75
Doalbears, --- 24
Doan, Clarissa M. 69
Dodge, Betsey E. 65
  Celina 18
  Martha C. 46
  Samantha 33
Dorland, Maria 9
Dorman, Eliza 29
Dotay, Mary Ann 56
  Phebe Ann 20
Douglass, Abigail 52
  Amanda 49
  Archibald 7, 11, 23, 67
  Catharine 23
  Hannah 67
  Jane 11
  Lydia 67
  Mary 7
Dove, Ann 58
Dowin, Mary 54
Downer, Diana 25
  Sophie L. 64
Downey, Frances Ann 41
Drake, Eliza Emeline 46
  Susan 38
Driscoll, Maria 67
Duel, Danny 5
Duguid, Alicia 86
Dummitt, Mary 43
Dunbar, Helen M. 31
  N. W. 20
Duncan, Cathia 60
  Lydia 60

Dunham, Almira 36
  Mary 74
Dunlap, Maria 84
Dunscomb, Nancy 45
Duvant, M. 51
Dyer, Edward 56
  Esther L. 58
  Louisa M. 60
  Sibil 56

Earll, Charlotte C. 2
  Clarissa Caroline 60, 84
  Elizabeth A. 68
  Hezekiah 15
  Hezikiah 11
  Jonas 60
  Julia M. 11
  Mary 17
  Matilda 15
  N. H. 68
  Nancy 17
  Sophroney 44
  Ulyssa 66
Eastman, Lydia 33, 78
Eaton, Mary Ann 6
  Sophronia 13
Eddy, Mary Jane 63
  Sarah E. 47
Edwards, Adelia L. 57
  Alanson 11, 27
  Clarissa 65
  Electa 6, 11
  Elizabeth L. 31
  Emily 76
  Frances M. 13
  Hannah 68
  Harriet 27
  Harriet A. 52
  Jane R. 29
  Julia 59
  Samuel 52
  Samuel L. 76
  Simeon 6
Eggleston, Ann Maria 8
  Benjamin 19, 53, 69

Eggleston, Catherine 19
  John B. 18
  Lovina 18
  Rebecca 69
  Sarah 53
Elder, M. A. 55
Eldridge, Barbara 18
Elliott, E. Ann 54
  Ursula Ann 28
Ellis, --- (Gen.) 18
  Electa 60
  Harriet 18
  Jane A. 61
  Nancy 60
  Sarah J. 6
Ellsbury, Dinah 43
Elsbury, Cornelia L. 63
  Harriet 19
Elsworth, Tryphena 5
Elwood, Catherine 26
Emmons, Nancy A. 4
English, Rebecca 63
Eno, Melissa 21
Enos, Phebe 15
  Polly 31
Evans, Esther E. 65
  Mary Ann 21
  Sarah L. 22
Everetts, Lydia 67

Fairbank, Sarah 78
Fairchild, --- (Rev. Mr.) 72
Fairman, Miranda 52
Fancher, Jane 72
Farmer, Sally Angelina 67
Farnham, Anna 52
  Emily 58
  R. 58
Farr, Mary Ann 74
Fay, Armelle P. 57
  Cornelia B. 54
  Electa 20
  James 54
  Maria 64
Fellows, Almira 27

Ferguson, Mary Ann 2
Ferris, Sarah 35
Field, Albert 59
  Emeline 59
Fields, Mary 55
  Sabrina 65
Fife, Clementine 48
Fillmore, William 77
Finch, Rosanna 11
Finn, Mary A. 67
Fish, Hannah 61
  Isabella 24
  Sarah Elizabeth 20
Fitch, Charlotte Augusta 68
  Harry 68
  Lydia P. 61
Fletcher, Ann 59
  Charity 35
  Joseph 59
Flint, Mary 36
  Philip 36
Fobbes, Annie 37
  John G. 37
Follet, Eliza 49
Folts, Elizabeth 78
Foot, Electa 74
  Laura 62
  Phebe Maria 66
Foote, Amanda L. 45
Forbes, Annie 37
Forbush, Dorinska 11
Ford, Emma 17
  Genet P. 12
  Louisa 34
  Lydia M. 51
  Martin 34
  Mary 64
Forman, Helen 67
  Joshua 22, 41, 67
  Margaret 22
  Mary E. 41
Forncrook, Louisa 16
Fort, Eleanor 13
Foster, Ann 60
  Ann E. 57
  Hannah A. 52
  Harriet 33
  Sally A. 65
Fowler, Augustus 50

Fowler, John 63
  Matilda B. 63
  Sarah Elizabeth 50
  Sarah M. 66
Fox, Harriet 55
  Sally 83
Francis, Cornelia 36
  David 49
  Emily 63
  Harriet L. 49
  Nancy J. 49
  Samuel 36, 63, 77
Fraser, John 47
  Margaret 47
Frashur, Huldah 17
  John 17
Frazer, Catherine 53
Frazier, Maria 54
Frederick, Jacob 60
  Lucetta 60
French, Helen Jane 55
  S. 55
  Theresa 80
Fries, Mary A. 41
Frink, Caroline 13
Frizell, Martha 78
Frost, Ann 67
  Matilda Louise 57
  Russell 12, 57, 67
  Sarah E. 12
Fryer, Catherine Maria 67
Fuller, --- (Mrs.) 14
  J. C. 30
  Jane 1
  Mary 33, 61
  Mary Ann 30
  Sarah 28
  Sophronia 1
  Susan 26
Fulton, Charlotte Ann 2
  Robert C. 21
  Sarah L. 21
Furman, --- 34
  Hannah 40
Furnace, Hannah 63

G

Gage, Eunice 31
  Lucy 9
Gallup, Martha 29
Galusha, Catharine Frances 54
  Ezra 54
Gambell, E. 64
  Lucy E. 64
Gardiner, Andalucia 57
Gardner, --- (Elder) 26
  Hannah 31, 55
  Lodusky 59
  Louisa 58
  Minerva 55
  Sarah 26
  Sarah Ann 2
  Sylvester 2, 55
Garlick, Mary E. 62
Garlock, Harriet 63
Gates, Anne 8
Gaumaer, Margaret 23
Gaylord, Chauncey 19
  Electa M. 8
  Hannah 19
  Harriet 2
  Lucretia 50
Geddes, James 5
  Laura 5
George, --- 30
Gibbs, Amanda 14
  Ann Eliza 26
  Eliza 26
  Maria L. 51
Gibson, Susan 63
Giddings, Mary M. 75
Gidney, Sally Ann 57
Gifford, Henry 28
  Mary E. 28
  Rebecca 47
  Susan 76
Gilbert, Ellen M. 51
  Harriet H. 6
  Hiram 63, 77
  Nancy C. 63
  Sarah 10
  Theodosia 15

Gillespie, Hugh 77
Gilmore, Isabel 75
Gilson, --- (Rev. Mr.) 74, 76, 83
  Sally 78
Glass, Martha J. 56
Godard, Maria 68
Goddwin, Maria Louise 15
Gold, Helen 36
Goodard, Caroline 9
Goodell, Evalina M. 61
  Mary 13
Goodrich, Almira 50
  Eliza C. 66
  Hannah 84
Goodsell, Laura 46
Goodwin, Emeline 77
  Marcus 39
  Maria Louise 15
  Ruama 39
Gordon, Jerusha 65
Gott, Ann B. 68
  Daniel 68
Gould, Beulah 40
  Julia 42
  Phares 42
Gray, Emeline P. 14
Greaves, Cynthia 10
Green, Laura 20
  Lucretia 1
Greene, Matilda 66
Greenfield, Amy 19
Greenman, Helen M. 44
  S. H. 44
Grennel, Ann Julia 49
Gridley, Sarah 50
Griffen, Lucy 40
Griffin, Lucinda A. 1
  Mary Ann 66
  Mary Jane 54
  Nancy D. 53
  Philinda 38
  Thirza L. 4
Grimes, A. E. (Mrs.) 27
Griswold, Horace 30
  Mary 30
Grooms, Harriet 59
Grossett, Zipporah T. 69
Grove, Cynthia 10

Grover, Lucy 25
Guiteau, Annah 59
Gumaer, Sally 38
Gunn, Elmira 51
 Sarah 83
Gurley, Emily 86
Gurnee, Louisa 64

Hadley, Mary Elizabeth 78
Hadox, Eliza 62
 Elizabeth 62
Hager, Adeline 12
 Milly 45
Haig, Harriet 58
Haines, Lydia 23
Hale, Lucinda 7
Hall, Adaline 63
 Caroline A. 7
 Clarissa 35
 Hannah B. 36
 Harriet 13, 74
 Harriet S. 26
 James 63
 Lucinda 15
 Lydia Jane 65
 Milicent 31
 Nancy 45
 Patty 33
 Ralph 7, 26
 Rhoda 2
 Sophia 12, 50
Halle, Sarah 55
Halstead, Martha Jane 23
Halt, Mary E. 40
Ham, Catharine 79
Hamilton, Betsey 75
 Leura 80
 Mary 78
 Phebe 37
 Washington 78
Hamlin, Mary 60
Hammond, Ann Eliza 72
 Julia A. 53
Hanchest, Mahaly 17
Hanchett, John 56

Hanchett, Lucy Maria 56
Hancock, Huldah 4
Hanks, Juliet 35
Hannum, Harriet 23
 Joanna 47
Hard, Luck 26
Hardy, Weltha A. 25
Hare, Sarah 40
Harle, Harriet 16
Harlow, Sophia 46
Harris, Abby J. 51
 Prudence 45
 Rebecca 43
Harrison, Mary C. 52
Hart, Caroline 60
 Cornelia C. 44
 Ephraim 44
 Lucy 1
 Richard P. 60
 Samuel 1
Harvey, Charlotte 19
 Harriet 20
Haskill, Philena 4
Haskins, Alson G. 39
 George 39
 Julia 8
 Matilda 5
Hatch, Betsey 6
 Diadama 10, 73
 Emeline 43
 Polly 58
 Tryphena 2
Haurl, Eliza 14
Haven, Sarah 56
Hawke, Mary 29
Hawkins, Sally 73
Hawley, Mary 42
 Matilda 65
Hayden, Sophronia C. 58
Haydon, Allen 54
 Helen Louisa M. 54
Hayes, Isabella 68
Hayler, Harriet 28
Haynes, Polly 27
Hays, Mary 66
Hazelton, Salley 84
Hazen, Horace 44
 Mary F. 44
Healy, Orpha 32

Heath, Mary A. 17
Hebard, Eunice 25
Hecock, Frances 26
Heed, Angeline L. 51
Helford, Catherine 63
Hempsted, Hannah 1
  William 1
Henderson, Ellen 42
  Laura 22
Henningan, Diadama 59
Henry, Andrew 62
  Ann 52
  Meriam 62
Herrick, Harriet J. 55
Herring, Julia 6
Hervey, Caroline 18
Hess, Laura Louisa 55
  Mary Elizabeth 7
  R. L. 55
Hewes, Louisa J. 64
Hewett, Jane 35
Hewson, Henrietta E. 53
Hickock, Jane Ann 65
  Morehouse 65
Hickok, Maria 30
Hickox, Ruah 27
Hicks, Amy 58
  Betsey Ann 49
  Henrietta 40
  Mary A. 14
Higby, Julia E. 24
Higgins, Julia Ann 67
  Mary H. 57
  Mercy H. 57
  Phoebe 5
Hight, Elizabeth C. 55
Higley, Ellen M. 9
  Emily 67
  Homer 9
Hill, Almira 59
  Charles 25
  Electa M. 47
  Sarah S. 25
  Susan 15
  Susan B. 66
Hillebert, Charlotte 50
Hilliard, Carolina Matilda 54
  William 54
Hillman, Sally 16

Hinckley, Sarah J. 58
Hine, Mary 75
  Sarah M. 56
Hinman, Harriet A. 68
  Maria 56
Hinsdale, Harriet 5
  Moses H. 5, 66
  Polly 66
Hitchcock, Manly 39
  Mary E. 39
  Samuel 53
  Sarah 60
  Wealthy 53
Hoag, Emily J. 53
Hobart, Orrilla 86
Hodge, Elizabeth 74
  R. W. 76
Holden, Elzina 23
  Harriet M. 34
Hole, Ann 24
Holley, G. 13
Holliday, Martha 38
Hollister, --- (Rev. Mr.) 77
  A. S. 75, 78, 84
Holobird, Addie L. 39
  N. S. 39
Homes, Euphemia 56
  Jane A. 38
Hooper, Caroline 41
  Pontius 41
Hopkins, --- (Dr.) 20
  Annie 49
  Caroline Louise 20
  Charlotte A. 7
  Hezekiah 7
  Mary 30
  Sophia 10
Hopper, Caroline N. 52
Horton, Mary Hane 57
Hotchkiss, Martha A. 68
Hough, P. B. 7, 37
Houghtaling, Nancy 80
  Phebe 39
  William I. 78
Hovey, Alfred 17
  E. 39
  Florence 17
  Permelia 85
How, Amaziah 32

How, Hannah Ann 17
  Minerva 32
  Samuel 17
Howard, Julia M. 39
  Olive H. 65
  Rosannah B. 85
Howe, Addison 36
  Asenath 22
  Eliza I. 53
  Huldah 51
  Mary E. 36
  Sally 59
  Sarah 59
Howell, Henrietta D. B. 29
  Martha 52
  Nancy 85
Howland, Mary Ann 49
  Perry 49
Howlett, Celestia C. 57
  Parley 57
Hoxie, Joseph 46
  Rokie 60
  Sarah 46
Hoyt, Elizabeth 76
  Esther Ann 17
Hubbard, Daniel 78
Huff, Abigail 78
Hughes, Sophia 86
Hume, Letitia 48
Humphrey, Adaline A. 49
  Arnold 60
  Clarinda 51
  Eliza A. 60
  Emeline 35
  Harriet 64
  Roana 11
Hunsiker, --- (Dr.) 63
  Kate Estelle 63
Hunt, Harriet 62
  Joyce 32
Hunter, Malinda M. 82
  Margaret 35
Huntington, George 60
  Hannah I. 60
  Israel 64
  Susan A. 64
Hurd, Sophronia 62
Hutchens, Louisa 49
  Margaret 63

Hutchins, Jane 44
Hutchinson, --- (Gen.) 62
  Betsey 50
  Elizabeth 17
  Lucia 42
  Lucy 32
  Sarah 9, 62
Huxtable, Martha E. 30
  Mary Jane 34
  Richard 30
Hyde, Mary Ann 4
Hydon, Mary 25

J

Ingalls, Fanny 25
Ingersoll, Sarah 21
Irwin, Jane 69
  Maria 14
Isdell, Emily 24

J

Jackson, Catherine 68
  Charles 27
  Clarissa Ann 36
  Malvina 27
Jacoby, Mary 38
James, Charlotte A. 73
  Lavina L. 43
  Polly 68
Jeffers, Eliza 58
Jenkins, Lydia 52
Jennigs, Polly 78
Jennings, Abigail 32
Jermaine, Margaret 60
Jerome, Harriet 8
  Ira 52
  Jane Helen 52
  John G., Forbes 37
Johnson, Ebenezer 48
  Electa 41
  John N. 32
  Margaret 60
  Maria 18

Johnson, Mary 32, 48
  Rebecca 13
  Rowana 66
  S. A. 57
Jones, Annis 6
  Betsey 65
  Eliza 48
  Jane 27
  Lucinda 3, 72
  Lucy 56
  Lurinda 3, 72
  Polly 78
Judd, Ansel 81
  Clarissa 81
June, Augusta P. 6

Kasson, Ambrose 53
  Frances 42
  Jane A. 53
  Jane Ann 82
Kean, Ebenezer 79
Keeler, Julia A. 68
  R. 68
Keeney, Susan M. 17
Kelderhouse, Lydia Ann 19
Keller, Huldah 9
Kellog, D. (Mrs.) 41
  Ruth 37
  Sarah 8
  Susan 46
Kellogg, Augustus 44
  Charlotte 48, 67
  D. 18
  Daniel 18
  Maria 18
  Mary Ann 18
Kelly, Eunice 47
Kendall, Percy 15
Kennedy, A. F. 51
  George 61
  Penelope 61
Kenyon, Charlotte L. 59
  Elizabeth A. 43
Kern, Caroline 32
Ketcham, --- (Miss) 85

Ketchum, Elizabeth 69
  Sallie 69
Keyes, Charlotte 67
  Elnathan 67
Kibby, Patty 65
Kilborn, Elizabeth 53
Kimball, Susan L. 63
Kind, Orphena 9
King, Amanda 53
  Henry F. 25
  Laury 63
  Lucinda 74
  Mary 61
  Mary Viall 25
  P. 61
Kingsley, Emily 62
  Lucy A. 67
  Sarah A. 27
Kinkaid, Betsey 61
Kinne, Eliza Kennet 3
  Polly 69
Kinney, Amelia J. 35
  M. A. 35
  Mary J. 37
  Olive 16
Kinyon, Hannah 65
Kirkpatrick, Rachel 59
Knapp, Amelia 56
  Betsey Ann 5
  Caroline Frances 23
  Castia 74
  Cornelia 74
  Eunice Ann 38
  Minerva 51
  Olive 85
  Polly 17
Kneeland, Amasa 8, 59
  Mary 59
  Stella 8
Knowles, Angelina 68
  Charlotte 26
Knowlton, Mary D. 12
  R. W. 16
  W. H. 12
Kruger, Daniel 29
  Eliza M. 29

Laberteau, Eliza Jane 67
Laberteaux, Affa 54
Ladd, Margaret 36
Ladue, Sally 59
Lake, Elder 85
Lamb, Josephine E. 66
Lamson, Sarah C. 47
Landon, Polly 13
Landsey, Sarah Ann 54
Lane, Fidelia R. 54
Lanes, Alicia 41
Langworthy, Lucinda 68
Lansing, --- (Rev. Dr.) 33
  Jacob 67
  Laura H. 33
  Minerva 67
Larkin, Elizabeth 34
Lathrop, Eliza 40
  Emma L. 9
  R. E. 9
Laton, Sarah 36
Lawnsbury, Elizabeth 6, 72
Lawrence, Ariel 46
  Asenath 46
  Bigelow 46
  Caroline 66
  Charlotte E. 60
  Eliza 42
  Fannie M. 35
  Gardner 35
  Grove 60
  Irene 55
  James R. 42, 58
  Joseph R. 55
  Lorette A. 57
  Margaret 58, 65
  Matilda 62
  Ruth 73
  Sally 55
Lawton, Abner 67
  Julia 67
  Julia A. 50
Leach, Clarissa 2
  Emeline 57
  Polly 64

Leavenworth, Clara 63
  John 63
LeBarron, Harriet 55
  Lorana 63
Lee, Harriet 12
  Jane 65
  Levi 65
  Phebe 21
  Sally 64
Legg, Emma 20
  Eunice A. 7
  John 63
  Juliet 56
  Juliette 63
  Louisa L. 54
  William 7
Leomonier, --- (Judge) 50
  Sally 50
Leonard, Ann S. 5
  David H. 5
  Jeanette 34
LeRoy, Caroline 66
  H. 66
Leslie, Helen 43
Lester, Eleanor 55
Letchworth, Hannah Maria 40
  J. 40
Lewis, Diantha 49
  Hannah E. 41
  John R. 41
  Mary A. 48
  Roxey 40
  Sophronia 77
Leynes, Alicia 41
Litherland, Charity 7
  Rebecca 7
  Samuel 7
Littlefield, Jane 16
Livingston, Adele C. 58
  J. W. 58
Long, Melinda 61
  Nancy L. 42
Longstreet, Elizabeth 64
Loomis, Amanda 19
Lord, Electa 61
  Melissa 61
Loss, Mary Maria 63
  Thankful 55
Loun, Mary 64

Lovejoy, Hannah 42
Loveless, Lucretia 58
 Nancy 57
Lownsbury, Elizabeth 6
Lowry, Rosanna 64
 William 64
Lyman, D. C. 39
Lynch, Ellen 1
 Maria 38
 Mary J. 51
Lynd, Jane 42
Lynes, Tamar 45
Lyon, Abigail G. 57
 Lucy 55

M'Enlear, Mary Ann 85
Mack, Betsey 12
Madison, Olive 4
Manchester, Alice 80
 Sarah Ann 61, 84
Mann, Harriet 27
Marble, Adeline 41
Maria, Eggleston 52
Marks, Betsey 14
Marsh, Abigail 20
 Betsey Ann 9
 Catharine 44
 Lynds 80
 Mary 81
Martin, --- (Mrs.) 81
 Angeline 16
Mason, Adeline 2
 R. B. 35
 Sarah 33
Mastin, Eliza 32
Mathews, John 14
 Mary 14
McCan, Bridget 22
McComby, Melinda 39
McComley, Melinda 39
McCormick, Catharine 16
McDonald, Nancy 16
McDougall, Margaret 38
McKibbett, Jane 27
Mead, Betsey P. 22

Mead, Philander 38
 Rebecca 1
 Sophia Ann 38
Mellen, Julia A. 25
 Lucius 25
Merriam, C. R. 19
 Emily 19
 Harriet T. 23
Merrian, Polly 42
Merrick, Calista 34
 Danforth 34
 Letitia 23
Merrill, Charlotte C. 25
 Mary Ann 47
 Ruth 10, 11
Merritt, Maria A. 11
Messinger, Polly 74
Miles, Harriet 32
Miller, Flora E. 78
 Sarah 3
 Sophia 22, 73
Mills, --- (Rev. Dr.) 18
 Ann Maria 18
 Louisa 16
 Marietta A. 31
 Mary Eliza 32
 Myron L. 32
Mitchell, Lucinda 43
Monk, Elsie 45
Montague, Mary A. 7
Moon, Abigail 12
More, Ann M. 8
Morehouse, Niram 81
Morey, Patty 6
Morgan, Calaphonia 11
 Christopher 5
 Cornelia L. 5
 Harriet E. 18
 Julia 33
 Lucinda 36
 Peter B. 18
 William 36
Morrison, Almira C. 3
Morse, Ann Eliza 25, 76
 Cornelia 16, 74
 Hannah 76
 Mary 32, 45
 William 25
Morton, C. 73, 74, 76, 78, 85

Morton, Margaret 1
Moseley, Charles 81
Mosely, Thomas 81
Moses, Alvira 46
  Charlotte 37
  Curtis 37
Mosley, Daniel 51
Mott, Susan 1
Muchmore, Martha 72
Mumford, Mary 21
  Thomas 21
Munroe, Cynthia 8
Murray, Jane 25
Myrick, Sarah 10

Naracong, --- 17
Nash, Caroline S. 28
Nelson, Seth 45
  Sophia A. 45
Nemmett, A. P. 62
  Eliza 62
Nettleton, Eliza A. 38
Newell, Harriet 44
Newton, Alminta 18
  Nancy A. 31
Nichols, Ann 7
Nickerson, Daniel 33
  Ruth 33
Nims, A. 61, 78, 83
Noble, Minerva 30
Nolton, Aurelia L. 16
Norman, Esther 3, 72
North, Phebe 12
Northon, Sarah 13
Nye, Remembrance 24

O'Sullivan, Margaret 20
Oakley, Eliza 2
Ogden, Martha B. 21
Oliver, Patty 1
Orr, Mary 14
Osborn, Cynthia Ann 37

Osborn, Emily H. 44
Ostrander, Elizabeth 44
Out, Maria 48
Owen, Louisa 36
  Lydia 5
  Sarah 34

Paddock, Hannah 10
  Samantha 81
Page, Chloe 15
Pain, John (Mrs.) 16
Palmer, Julia 16
  Louisa 2
Pardee, Emily J. 3
Parent, Elvira 16
Parish, Phebe Ann 29
Parker, Amanda 19
  Enos 82
  Lewis 9
  Mary 32
  Mary Taylor 9
  Sarah Ann 2
Parkhurst, Elizabeth 12
Parks, Jane 31
  Laura 79
Parlor, Grace 83
Parmeter, Aurelia Maria 26
  Sylvia 38
Parsons, Abby 10
  Adaline C. 47
  Anna R. 33
  Bishop N. 21
  Clara 21
  Esther W. 16
  Florilla 15
  Gould 47
  H. Janette 39
  Levi 13, 33
  Mary Abigail 13
Partridge, Charlotte 23
Pattee, Hannah 40
Patten, Emily 80
Peacock, Caroline N. 43
  William R. 43
Peake, Mary Ann 80

Pease, Amanda 6, 72
  Eugenia 15
  James 15
  Minerva R. 17
Peck, Julia Ann 6
  Juliet 33
  Louisa H. 32
  Lydia 24
  Mary 8
  Phebe 37
Peckham, Eliza 7
Pellse, Helen 20
Penny, Emily 23
Perkins, Betsey 30
Perry, Fanny 76
Phelps, Abigail 74
  Matilda 14
Philips, Maria E. 79
Phillips, --- (Miss) 82
  Caroline 12
  Elijah 10, 82
  Esther A. 10
  Freelove 30
  Mary 35
Pickett, Joanna 28
Pickle, Nancy 15
Pierce, Catharine 29
Pierson, Ruth 34
Pinchler, Ann 43
Platt, Abigail G. 3
  Daniel 3
Plympton, Mary 24
Pollock, Cordelia 19
Pomeroy, Mary 29
Pond, Almira 48
Port, J. G. 51
Porter, --- (Rev. Mr.) 72, 73, 82
  Elizabeth Townsend 6
  James 6, 55
  M. 78
  Maria H. 31
  Mary E. 13
  Samuel 31
Post, Helen 77
Potter, Amelia 46
  David 82
  Loretta 1
  Melvina 42

Potter, Nicholas 46
Powers, John 29
  Mary Ann 29
Pratt, Cynthia 11
  Helen C. 7
  Luther 55
  Manoah 7
Prentice, Lydia 28
Preston, --- (Deacon) 15
  Mary Ann 15
Price, Genet 18
Prindle, Minerva 46
Pulsifer, Ann 15
Purchase, Mary A. 33
Putnam, Olive 36

Queen, Elizabeth 41

Radford, Marianne 37
Rand, Harriet N. 18
  M. L. (Mrs.) 13
Randall, Julia 2
  Mariette 8
Randolph, M. L. (Mrs.) 13
Rawling, Emma 46
Raymond, Amy 39
  Martha 32
Recard, Fidelia M. 10
Redfield, Caroline A. 48
  L. H. 48
Reed, Andrew 23
  Charlotte P. 30
  Juliette 28
  Mary 23
  Samantha 16
  Sarah 15
  Thomas 28
Reeves, Jane 37
Remington, Nancy M. 37
Reynolds, Cornelia A. 43
  Harriet 25

Reynolds, Ira J. 21
　Lucyette 21
Reynor, Hannah 34
Rhoades, --- 29
　Alzina 47
　Cornelia 26
　Frances S. 43
　Hannah F. 13
　Harvey 43
　Jane 3
　Joseph 82
　Lois 83
　Sarah S. 78
Rhodes, Cyrus 13
　Esther 7
　Mary E. 13
　Sarah 33
Rice, Emily 11
Ricer, Angeline 19
Rich, Jane 42
Richards, Esther M. 14
　Fannie Jewett 34
Richardson, Adeline 44
　Catherine 7
　J. L. 7
　Julia A. 29
Richmond, Sybil E. 20
Riddle, Eliza 42
　John 42
Rishmore, Elizabeth 33
Robbins, Ann 38
　E. 37
　Matilda 37
Roberts, Wealthy 76
Robinson, Amelia 14, 19
　H. 10
　Hannah 4
　John W. 19
　Margaret D. 10
　Roxena 31
　Sarah Ann 26
　Susan 7
Rockwell, Sarah E. 4
Roe, Sally M. 9
Rogers, Betsey 35
　Lucy 80
Root, Abigail N. 10
　Eliza 28
　Harriet 33

Ross, Ichabod 27
　Mary E. 27
Roudley, Mary 18
Roulet, John S. 83
Rouley, C. S. 24
　P. C. 24
Rouse, Mary Jane 17
Row, Barbara 32
Rowe, Mary Ann 36
Rowley, E. 35
　Frances 35
　Sally 47
Ruff, Mary Ann 43
Ruggles, Elizabeth 27
Rumsey, Selina 23
Russell, E. A. 23
　Elizabeth 27
　Emily 79
　Lucinda 14
　Mary Osborne 23
　Salley 83
Rust, Helen M. 4
　P. N. 4

Sabin, John 45
　Mary 45
Sackett, Fanny 23
　Sarah 9
　William A. 23
Safford, Clarinda 73
　Elizabeth 40
Sage, Alvira 76
Sampman, Catharine 17
Sandford, Harriet M. 1
　Lucy 23
Sandiforth, Harriet 43
Sanford, --- (Judge) 13
　Laura P. 13
　Sally N. 30
Savage, Moses B. 83
Schuff, June 18
Scoville, Anna 37
　Mary Ann 7
　Sally 10
Scranton, Lyman 32

Scranton, Mary Adaline 32
Searl, Hannah 45
 Heman 45
Sedgewick, Ann 32
Seelay, James 72
Seely, Clarissa 21, 75
 Helen 5
Selkreg, James 80
Selkrig, James 74, 75, 86
Sellick, Delia A. 31
Selover, Hannah 9
Severn, Henry 34
 Sarah Jane 34
Seymour, Laura Jane 47
 Maria 83
 Miles 47
Shave, Betsey Ann 31
Shaver, Lucy 78
Shaw, Maria J. 28
Sheldon, Rosina 48
 Sarah S. 36
 Susan 39
Shelton, Ann Marie 38
Shepard, Susan 20
Shepherd, Frances 35
 Phebe Ann 22
Sherman, Elizabeth 44
 Lottie F. 12
 Rebecca W. 3
 Sally A. 79
Sherwood, Eliza 6
 Isaac 6
 Margaret 13
 Martha 77
Shumway, Sarah 5
Simmons, Mary 47
 Nancy 45
Simons, George 84
Singerland, Philena 38
Sixbury, Delany 84
Skeels, Rhoda 14
Slade, Almira 84
 Olive 64
Slocum, Elizabeth 81
 Mary Ann 9
Smith, --- (Rev. Mr.) 75, 83, 84, 85
 Adeline R. 44
 Amy 34

Smith, Ann E. 22
 Benoni 16
 Charles 79
 Deborah A. 16
 Elizabeth 19, 22
 Ellen 65
 Emeline 25
 Freelove (Mrs.) 8
 Hannah 3
 Hannibal 23
 Harding 65
 Harriet 85
 J. H. (Mrs.) 35
 Josiah 38
 Julia 29
 Julia E. 22
 Louisa 4
 Maria A. 16
 Maria E. 23
 Mary 25
 Matilda A. 41
 Mehitabel Ann 19
 Nancy 47
 R. U. 37
 Rosetta R. 37
 Sarah 48
 Sarah E. 65
 Sarah M. 38
 Wealthy 14
 William 14
Snook, Harriet 8
 John 8, 30
 Mary 30
 Matilda 30
Snyder, --- (Rev. Mr.) 83
 E. J. (Mrs.) 1
Souls, Lydia 80
Southard, Angeline 9
Spafford, Eureka 46
 Horatio G. 46
Spalding, George 11
 Mayette 11
 Sarah 35
Sparks, Eliza 34
 Julia 33
Spaulding, Fanny W. 20
 George 20
 Prudence 34
Spears, Margaret 74

Spencer, Ann 19
 Catherine Mary 31
 Delina M. 37
 John 19, 31
Sprague, Aurilla 86
Springer, Benjamin 16
 Desire L. 16
St. John, Dorothy 41
Stanton, Lucretia 9
 N. P. 84
Staring, Rhoda 4
Starr, Sophia 2
Stearns, Cornelia Bradley 25
 J. 25
Stebbins, Nancy A. 8
Steele, Electa 2
Stevens, Hannah E. 1
 John L. 1
 Maria E. 32
Steward, Cynthia 39
Stillson, Christiana 84
 Eli L. 84
Stockwell, P. J. 9
Stolp, Hannah L. 28
 Lydia E. 40
 Rebecca 18
Stone, Eliza Jane 44
 Sarah Fine Emeline 79
Stoner, Christine L. 9
 Nancy 28
Story, --- 36
Stout, Laura 74
Strobeck, Mary E. 5
Strong, Emma 23
 Harriet 45
 Janet 27
 Oliver R. 27, 45
 Sarah C. 21
Sunderland, Ann 13
Sutherland, Ann 13
Sutphen, May Jane 17
Swan, Nancy 23
Sweeing, Clarissa 9
Sweet, Charles W. 10
 Mary 10
 Philura 82
Sweeting, Judah 28

T

Tabor, Elizabeth 20
Taft, Sally Ann 4
Tarbox, Maria 8
Taylor, Christiana 29
 Frances 3
 G. L. 86
 Maria 33
 Mary Jane 23
 Olive 18
 Phebe 83
 Polly Mary 42
Teall, Oliver 31
 Phebe A. 31
Tefft, Chloe 43
Teneur, --- 28
Terry, Amanda 21
 Erastus 21
 Frances 31
 Ginnet 40
 Jane Ellen 14
 Marion 29
 Ruhama A. 2
Terwilliger, Eliza 9
Thomas, Maria 36
 Sophronia 18
 William 36
Thompson, Elizabeth Ann 6
 Jane 48
 Mary B. 10
 Peter 10
Thorn, Mary Ann 11
Thorout, Susan 41
Tibbals, Daniel 77
 Mary Ann 77
Tiffany, Eveline 25
Tillotson, Orange S. 3
Tinkham, Charlotte 4
Todd, Laura A. 18
Toles, Maria 12
Tomkins, Delia 9
Tompkins, Adeline Orilda 21
Tonkin, Jessie M. 25
Topham, Louisa 8
Traffagan, Catharine 43
Treat, Almira Jane 5
Tripp, Roxena 33

Truesdell, Rosanna 30
Turbish, Mary Jane 14
Turner, Olive 19
Tuttle, Emily A. 41
  Jemimaette 27

Van Schaick, Cordelia 3
VanBethuysen, --- 7
VanBlaricum, Harriet 12
VanBuren, Eveline 24, 76
Vanderburgh, Jane A. 2
VanDewalker, Mary 32
VanEtte, Jacob 30
VanEtten, Huldah 30
VanHoosen, Keturah 30
VanKleek, --- 19
VanRanst, C. W. 46
  Susan Frances 46
VanSlyke, Eliza 40
VanTyne, B. F. 38
  Lydia Ann 38
VanValin, Mary Ann 26
VanVeghten, Alida 46
  John 46
Vedder, Maria G. 40
Veeder, Diana 7
Voorhees, J. E. 12
  Jane L. 12
Vosburgh, John 36
  Margaret 36
Vrooman, Sarah M. 25

Wadsworth, Sally 16
Waiser, Adelaide 17
Walch, Almira 33
Waldron, Margaret 27
Walker, Ruth 85
Wallace, Deborah B. 22
  Maria 28
  Sarah A. 39
Walton, Caroline 72

Walton, Julia 86
Ward, Lucy 77
  Mary Ann 14
  Rhoda A. 21
Warner, Amelia 17
  Ann 12
Watson, Caroline 30
  Daniel 25
  Elenora 25
  John 85
  Mariette 16
  Norman 16, 30
  R. P. 65
Wattles, Nancy 16
Way, Clarissa 31
  Rebecca Ann 24
Weaver, Clarina 19
  Clarissa 19
Webb, Helen M. 85
  James 22
  Mary A. 1
  Sally 83
  Susan 22
Webster, Amanda 1
  Emeline S. 36
  Emily 27
  Ephraim 1
Weed, Evalina T. 46
  Walter 46
Weeks, Elizabeth 20
Welch, --- 12
  Bridget 27
  Caroline 27
  Hester A. 45
  L. A. 11
  Maria 22
Weld, Keziah 76
  Zeziah (Keziah) 27
Wells, Jane A. 74
  Nancy 42
  Phebe 41
West, Almira 8
  Irene 5
  Mary A. 41
  Susan 21
Westlake, Maria 18
Weston, Polly 36
Wethey, Norissa 4
Wheadon, S. C. 66

Wheatley, Betsey A. 32
  Harriet 36
Wheaton, Betsey Maria 48
  Fannie A. 23
Wheeler, Amena 48
  Caroline 10
  Delia F. 20
  Frances 47
  Maria S. 4
  Olivia 81
  Thomas 20
Wheelock, Dorothy 80
White, Asa 46
  Caroline 46
  Helen N. 11
  Henrietta B. 37
  J. C. B. 11
  Peregrine 36
Whiting, Delia Ann 15
  Jane Elizabeth 29
Whitmore, Angelica 28
  Salley 19
Whitney, Abbey 38, 78
  Orpha 5
Whittaum, Margaret 38
Whittum, Mary 38
Wiborn, Almira 9
Wicks, Harriet 15
  Henrietta 40
Wilcox, Amanda 7
  Ann Dorinda 80
  Belinda 46
  Calista 77
  Frances R. 32
  Jane 5
  Mary 6
Wilkie, Mary 24
Wilkin, Bethiah 47
Wilkinson, Mary L. 14
Willard, Frances M. 38
Willetts, Latitia 2
  Valentine 2
Willey, Hannah 32
William, James 43
Williams, Alma C. 72
  Silas 86

Williams, Waty 22
Willington, Lucretia 15
Willsey, Ann 11
Wilsey, C. 35
Wilson, --- 7
  Joseph S. 25
  Mary S. 25
Wiltsie, Amy 15
  Elizabeth 17
Winchell, Amy 4
Winslow, Lucy 79
Wismore, Minerva P. 2
Wisner, Hannah 78
Withey, Harriet M. 41
Wood, Alica Ann 21
  Elizabeth 16
  Jane 40
  Maria 4
Woodbury, Juliet 30
Woodford, Esther H. 46
Woodward, Angeline 24
Woodworth, H. P. 44
  Mary Louise 44
Worden, Angelica 11
  James 86
  Maria 7
Worthing, Eliza K. 3
  J. 3
Wright, Jane 34
Wyckoff, Ann G. 21
  Ann Jennett 1
  Jonathan 1, 21
Wycoff, Jonathan 12
  Julia 12

Yarrington, Amanda 6
Yates, Mary 11
  Phebe 12
Yordon, Margaret 12
Young, --- (Judge) 21
  Mary F. 21
Youngs, Mary 45

Other books by Mary Keysor Meyer:

*A Directory of Cayuga County Residents Who Supported
Publication of the History of Cayuga County, New York*

*Abstracts from Madison County, New York Newspapers
in the Cazenovia Public Library*

Baltimore City Birth Records, 1865–1894

Cemetery Inscriptions of Madison County, New York, Volume 1
Mary K. Meyer and Joyce C. Scott

Divorces and Names Changed in Maryland by Act of the Legislature, 1634-1867

*Free Blacks in Harford, Somerset and
Talbot Counties, Maryland 1832*

*Meyer's Directory of Genealogical Societies in the U.S.A.
and Canada: 1998–2000, 12th Edition*
Family of Mary K. Meyer

*Westward of Fort Cumberland: Military Lots Set Off for
Maryland's Revolutionary Soldiers*

Who's Who in Genealogy and Heraldry 1990
Mary K. Meyer and P. William Filby

Other books by William M. Beauchamp:

*Revolutionary Soldiers Resident or Dying in Onondaga County, New York;
with a Supplementary List of Possible Veterans*

Supplement to Revolutionary Soldiers of Onondaga County, New York

Moravian Journal Relating to Central New York, 1745-1766

www.ingramcontent.com/pod-product-compliance
Lightning Source LLC
Chambersburg PA
CBHW071129090426
42736CB00012B/2067